User Experience Design

BASICS

DESIGN

Gavin Allanwood
Peter Beare

User Experience Design

A Practical Introduction

Second Edition

BLOOMSBURY VISUAL ARTS

LONDON · NEW YORK · OXFORD · NEW DELHI · SYDNEY

BLOOMSBURY VISUAL ARTS
Bloomsbury Publishing Plc
50 Bedford Square, London, WC1B 3DP, UK
1385 Broadway, New York, NY 10018, USA

BLOOMSBURY, BLOOMSBURY VISUAL ARTS and the Diana logo
are trademarks of Bloomsbury Publishing Plc

First published in Great Britain 2014
This edition published 2019

A catalogue record for this book is available from the British Library.

Library of Congress Cataloging-in-Publication Data
Names: Allanwood, Gavin, author. | Beare, Peter, 1970- author.
Title: User experience design : a practical introduction / Gavin Allanwood & Peter Beare.
Description: Second edition. | New York : Bloomsbury Publishing Plc, 2019. |
Series: Basics design | Includes bibliographical references and index.
Identifiers: LCCN 2018047122 (print) | LCCN 2018047460 (ebook) | ISBN 9781350021716 (Epdf) | ISBN
9781350021730 (Epub) | ISBN 9781350021709 (pbk. : alk. paper)
Subjects: LCSH: User interfaces (Computer systems)—Design. | Design—Human factors.
Classification: LCC QA76.9.U83 (ebook) | LCC QA76.9.U83 A45 2019 (print) | DDC 005.4/37—dc23
LC record available at https://lccn.loc.gov/2018047122

ISBNs: PB: 978-1-3500-2170-9
eBook: 978-1-3500-2173-0
ePDF: 978-1-3500-2171-6

Series: Basics Design

Typeset by Lachina Creative, Inc.
Printed and bound in China

To find out more about our authors and books visit
www.bloomsbury.com and sign up for our newsletter.

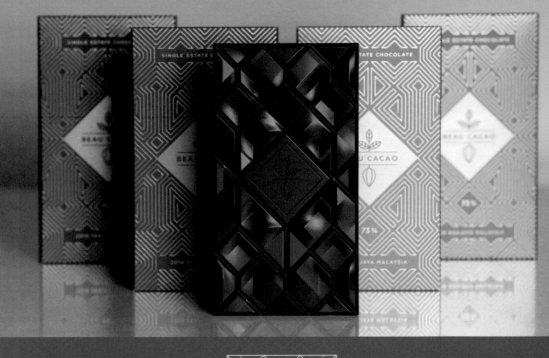

Contents

5

Design constraints 95

The online companion for this book offers easy access to learning resources for students and teachers of UX Design. The short link shown alongside this ◉ symbol can be entered into your web or mobile browser for direct access to further information and downloadable content.

6

Mindset and toolset 125

Figure 1 Frontispiece
Working with Beau Cacao, Adam Gill created an elegant design for their fine chocolate bars. As well as providing the practical grid to aid snapping of the bar, the tessellating pattern evokes the Malaysian origin of the ingredients. In the mould, an undulating specular surface to the bars is formed, stimulating the senses of touch and sight as well as taste. What factors has Adam controlled in order to change a commodity into a pleasurable experience?

12

LEARNING
ACTIVITIES

ACTIVITY	SKILL
11	Concept Sketching
7	Context Awareness
1,7	Creative Thinking
7	Creative Writing
3	Data Gathering
6	Design Testing with Users
1	Developing Empathy
2	Differentiation
2	Discovering User Characteristics
3	Ideation
8	Identifying User Goals
4,8	Interaction Architecture
4	Interaction Design
6,9	Interface Design
3,4	Interviewing
2,12	Iterative Design
1	Logic
11	Mapping
8,10	Mapping User Journeys
5	Measuring Emotional Affect
3,4	Notetaking
7	Objectivity
4	Observation
10	Onboarding
8	Problem Solving
12	Prototyping
3	Qualitative Research
4,5	Quantitative Research
1,2	Recognizing Diversity
8	Requirements Analysis
4	Scenario Building
5	Scientific Method
9	Seeing Design Patterns
1	Storytelling
11	Team Communication
12	Toolset Selection
2	User Research

Hey new reader! We are going to imagine for the moment that you are human being, sitting somewhere warm and comfortable having just made a nice cup of tea. In your hands you are holding a physical copy of our book and have opened it at this page for the first time. We wonder what you were expecting and why you are here. What were the chain of events that have led to this point? Could we have known about you and your motivations before you picked up the book? If we did could we have made the book even better? Of course, you may be reading this text on a screen or you may in fact be a robot, busily indexing and referencing our words for a machine to learn. Whoever you are – welcome!

The printed book is unlikely to spontaneously reorganize, change content or disappear without trace. It will not silently report your page turning to our publishers or grow dim and fade away as a battery dies. In the digital world such effects are common, and the ideas of infinite space, variability and connectedness are considered the new normal. Modern devices offer countless ways for designers to deliver, update and manage content for users. These awesome new powers of communication need to be applied with the consequential human experience in mind.

On the following pages the simple linear architecture of this book is presented as a graphic: a visual device that will help you to conceive the book's structure and recognize where it starts and where it ends. You can easily see the approximate position of particular pages and their relationship to others. If you hadn't read this short explanation you would most likely have understood all that without really thinking. If you are viewing the book online you could reasonably expect to be able to interact with the graphic, using it as a control for navigating the book's contents. The experience of each medium is different and you probably have a preference based on a comparison between them. Read on to find out what UX Designers do to make digital designs better for the people who use them.

Figure 2
You'll learn more by trying the twelve activities in this book. They offer a gentle introduction to the skill topics listed here.

Forematter / Contents / Overview / Introduction	Methods & Background	CH2. USERS	Fallibility	CH3. EXPERIENCE DESIGN	Simplicity
CH1. WHAT IS UXD?	Stakeholders	User Research	Expectation	Competitive Advantage	Challenge
Designing Interactive Experiences	Activity #2 Designing For Others	The User's World	Motivation	Brands	Gestalt Theory
Life's Experiences		Co-Experience	Activity #4 The Journey Concept	Productivity	Semiotics
Activity #1 The Big Picture		Activity #3 Listening and Learning		Activity #5 Quantifying Sentiment	Narrative
Roles in UX Design		Emotional Responses		Fun	Constraints
Today's Multi-Disciplinary Teams		Memory		Usability	Activity #6 Recognizing Intuition

Figure 3
The contents of this book presented as a simple graphic to help provide a simple overview and to encourage readers to dip in rather than progress in a linear fashion. Shorter activities are highlighted in the dotted green boxes.

This book is for you if you are learning about interactive design and plan to be involved in creating a product or service for other people to use. We aim to introduce you to a way of thinking that will help you see that excellence in design depends on more than just creative skills. By carefully considering the factors that combine to create a good user experience, your work will be more effective and ultimately much more rewarding.

The first edition of this book was published in 2014 and since then there has been a phenomenal shift towards user centred design. A clear understanding of UX Design methods is now a requirement for the majority of employment roles in digital design. Governments around the world, including the UK government, are setting clear service standards for those who wish to create publicly funded digital services. The service standards are very clear about the need to apply specific UX Design methods and so it is appropriate that they are referenced within this book.

We are happy that designers, project stakeholders and educators have all told us that they found the first edition to be just what they needed to understand the basic principles of the topic. This second edition will hopefully reinforce the message that UX Design is a way of thinking characterised by an empathic approach. The 'UX' tag communicates the message that 'we understand what it takes to give our users a good experience'. Perhaps because of its strong appeal, the UX tag has been erroneously applied in recruitment advertising to identify roles in visual interface design. The real strength of a UX approach is that it encourages all members of a project team, including interface designers, to work together to achieve results that provide the best achievable user experience.

Whether we like it or not, our daily lives now involve products and services accessed primarily through digital interfaces. Design teams who understand and can apply UX methods in constructing systems and interfaces will give their clients a strong competitive advantage. This fact alone will provide plenty of work for UX people well into the future.

There are six chapters and twelve activities, most of which can be completed without access to a computer. Together they combine to demystify the subject and help to provide you with the necessary foundation knowledge to start to apply a UX Design approach to your own work.

The first chapter will get you thinking about human experience in its broadest sense, and in following chapters you will learn about human factors, design theory and practical approaches to experience design. In the second half of the book we introduce methods and processes applied to achieve good results. Finally, we explore the tools available to UX Designers and explain how to prototype and iterate designs to evaluate and improve design decisions.

Figure 4
The view from inside this Tesla production car is an extreme example of how the driving experience has changed with advances in technology. It is an exciting and challenging time to be involved in creating designs that deliver great new user experiences in all aspects of our daily lives.

What is user experience design?

In this chapter, we explore the idea that human experience of the modern world is almost entirely influenced by human design. We expand on that idea and apply it to the field of interactive design, explaining how designers have adopted roles, built teams and applied multiple methods to improve their work. Modern UX Design practice is compared with other approaches and in the second activity we demonstrate how the focus for design can be stronger by identifying specific users and their context.

Designing interactive experiences

Products of UX Design include websites, mobile apps, voice interfaces, vehicle systems, games, tools and a host of devices used in industry and by consumers in their daily lives.

UX Design is a realistic approach to the process of designing digital products that require some sort of human interaction. If it were a doctrine then it would teach the need for knowledge, understanding, respect, empathy, purpose and productivity.

For a designer, the abiding rule is to strive to make the quality of the users' experience a top priority. The basic logic behind this approach can be simply explained by stating a truism; a successfully designed product is one that meets the requirements of its owner and provides a good experience for the intended users. Products that offer poor user experience will sooner or later be replaced by improved designs. Low-quality designs can have far reaching and potentially ruinous results for both the owner and the designer. With such high stakes it is not surprising that most companies now adopt a UX Design approach and many have established in-house teams to manage ongoing projects.

It is a big challenge to achieve a balance of what is good for the user and what can be accomplished within the constraints of time, budget and other resources. For this reason, successful UX Design teams need to be highly efficient. Most are multidisciplinary, including just the right number of people with a mix of expertise. Roles and responsibilities often overlap to add resilience to the team. A range of methods are applied to keep the process moving in the right direction. Each part of a product is tested with users to ensure that design objectives are being achieved and many final products undergo multiple revisions in their lifetime.

We think that there will always be more people needed to advocate UX Design. Perhaps you could become one of them?

'It's not enough that we build products that function, that are understandable and usable, we also need to build products that bring joy and excitement, pleasure and fun, and yes, beauty to people's lives.'
Donald Norman

Figure 5
Osmo is a games system which incorporates interactive software and a reflector which allows it to 'see' what is in front of it. The player manipulates tangible tools, blocks, and tokens to extend the gameplay beyond the confines of the touchscreen device into the environment of the player. Rich experiences like this require the collaboration of skilled individuals and teams with a deep understanding of technology and of human behaviour.

Life's experiences

If everything around you that is the product of a design process was taken away, what would remain? The climate defies our attempts to design its behaviour and so we create environments that protect us from it when needed. In almost every other respect, humans create the conditions that define our living experience.

Much of the quality of our life experience depends on the products of design that we encounter on our way. We have expectations, we make choices and, if we are lucky, we can choose how we want to live our lives. Our use of language, social trends and the development of culture evolve through human behaviour and social interaction. Designers need to consider the impact of their work on the people they are designing for and create work that shows an understanding of their needs.

As an individual designer, you will find yourself contributing to the universe of products of design. Your work may impact on small numbers of people, or on whole populations. You will want it to fit neatly into their lives and give them a good experience. If users can intuit meaning in your designs and achieve something without being made to think too hard then you have probably done a good job.

As part of a design team building an interface for an airline booking website you may be told that the main objective is to sell more tickets and increase your client's sales income. It should be made clear that your client in this scenario is the airline and not its customers. This distinction is important because the needs of the client and the needs of the client's customers are often quite different. A good UX team manages the tension between competing needs and works to achieve the best possible balance.

UX Designers ask fundamental questions about the context and motivation of potential customers. They need to know about the people who will use the website and what is required to provide them with a good user experience. Taking a wide view from the start they understand that air travel is part of a bigger scenario and is not usually the whole experience. They undertake research to see where their design fits into the user's life, asking questions like 'why are they travelling?', 'are they travelling alone?', 'what is their biggest fear?'

Undertaking user research reveals design challenges. In the case of airline seat booking, it may be discovered through research that more than 75% of travellers are a lot happier if they can see a seating plan of the aircraft and choose to book specific seats. To deliver such a requirement, a host of contributing design elements will need to work effectively for both the user and back-end data systems. At some point the requirement will need to be assessed to see if the potential user experience gains are achievable within the budget for the design. Only if the client can understand the potential benefits will the hard work of making the interface begin. This will include regular testing with users to make sure that the interface design actually provides the benefits expected.

Figure 6
This well-trodden coastal path fulfils the requirements of users to take a scenic route while avoiding obstacles and the cliff edge. In this case, the path does not precisely follow the cliff edge and so a balance has been achieved between the need to take in the sea view and the need to make reasonable progress. This is evidence of successful collaborative design providing a good experience without any apparent design process.

Activity #1

The big picture

This activity introduces the idea that your designs will form part of a much larger scenario for the people who use them. A world exists outside of any user interface that you construct. You need to research the user's context and observe them in their world. Right now, you do not have the time or the budget to do this, so here is a workable alternative.

Using storytelling you'll see how it is possible to gain initial insights and ideas that can help your design contribute to improving the user experience. This is a creative process fuelled by your imagination, your own experience, logic and common sense. It's a quick and relatively cheap way to discover the user's needs, prioritise design requirements and identify potential problems. Later on it will be necessary to validate any findings with real user research.

Start afresh. Keep away from the Internet, Google and existing airline interfaces. You'll need a pen, paper and a lot of imagination.

Steps

1 – scenario

A classic rock band are reuniting for one last tour. Erik, Martha and Zak want desperately to see them perform. The band have just released a range of tour dates in different cities in the US and Canada, starting in three months. Erik and Martha live in London (England) and Zak lives in Paris (France). Ideally, they would like to travel together. They are flexible on dates and want to choose the city venue that offers the best value for money.

2 – tell the story

Following the guidance below, write four paragraphs that tell the story of the trip. Alternatively, if you prefer brevity to prose then simply write lists instead of paragraphs.

What are the reasons these three travellers are organizing this trip together? (Remember - they don't exist. Use your imagination!)

Tell us who is organizing the trip. What have they written on their 'to-do' list? What are their priorities?

What could possibly go wrong? Write about aspects of the trip or the prior arrangements that could give the travellers a bad experience.

Using your new power of time travel, tell us about all the things that made the trip great, like the group selfie taken on the observation deck at the airport.

3 – identify features

Now, with this wealth of (fictional) background research available to you, write about the sort of features that a travel app could include. Remember that you are aiming to improve the user experience. As a first step you could think about reducing the chances of the things in Paragraph 3 from happening.

Hints

Small decisions, made early in the planning of the friends' trip could have a big impact on their experience later on. Making sure that everyone knows the travel schedule is obviously important. If Erik is organizing the trip then how does he reliably keep the others in the loop?

The booking system already knows about Martha and Zak. Perhaps the interface could provide the option to keep them updated. How will the design support this? It's clearly a priority that they that all get to the airport on time. Knowing about the airport's facilities could help the group find a good place to meet up and take that selfie . . .

⊙ uxto.me/a1

Figure 7
Selfies put humans in the foreground of any situation. They help designers connect emotionally with the people who use their products and services.

Roles in User Experience Design (UX)

In the preceding pages, we've described UX as an approach to design that makes it possible to achieve the goal of giving users a good experience. Traditional methods of design generally apply a linear 'conceive, design, build and test' process. Often the conceive stage is done behind closed doors and those responsible for the design stage are not able to request changes at the build stage. When the product reaches the final stage, tests are made to see if it works as expected. Sometimes the testing stage will happen after the product has reached the market and the test is simply to see if it is accepted by its users. If users reject it on the basis that it doesn't work and if the company has survived, the designers go 'back to the drawing board'. Unfortunately products that perform their function badly can continue to exist, even though they fail to consider the experience of the people who will use them.

UX Design offers a much more holistic approach, considering users from the start of a design idea and then applying the talents of a multidisciplinary group of people to achieve products that work really well. It is a particularly suitable approach to digital design because, unlike working with physical materials, there are more possibilities to test, refine and update products within a development cycle. Because it is an approach and not a well-defined procedure, it can be more difficult for design teams to adopt UX Design than more conventional methods.

For this reason, many design teams include a member who has a specific responsibility to ensure that UX Design happens. They will be enthusiastic supporters of the mission to achieve excellent user experiences, and they will ensure that everyone in the team understands the approach and the reasons behind it. As part of their role they will monitor and evaluate the success of the project and the costs involved, making sure that the approach provides a good return on investment as well as producing much better designs. To do this they will create an organizational framework, set ground rules, manage the scope of projects and referee meetings to ensure that uninformed opinion does not prevail.

In a large team, there are job titles that explicitly define the UX role as independent from any responsibility for production. These include:

UX Design Director

Strategist

User Evangelist

Analyst

In many projects, UX Design is a responsibility added to a development and production role such as:

UX Designer

UI Designer

Front-end Developer

Software Engineer

Employers often say they are looking for a 'team player' and by this they usually mean someone who will cooperate and communicate with the rest of the team. If your work is shrouded in mystery and you prefer to deliver a brainchild after weeks of solitary work in a hidden corner of the studio, then you will need to change your approach in order to be a successful player in a UX Design team.

Figure 8
There continues to be a strong demand for people with specific skills in one or more of the core UX Design roles.

Today's multidisciplinary teams

A multidisciplinary team is one that contains people of quite different backgrounds and skills who are brought together to work closely on a particular project. The 'discipline' part of 'multidisciplinary' provides a clue to some of the difficulties that teams encounter. When learning their skill or developing their expertise each member of the team will have disciplined themselves to focus on a particular area, develop specific knowledge and become skilled in specific techniques.

They will probably have done all this with a group of like-minded people who share a range of social and cultural ideas. This is good because we expect a systems engineer to work with precision to make things that are highly functional and efficient. We also expect a graphic designer to produce work that applies visual language to communicate ideas and meaning that can influence us on an emotional level.

A multidisciplinary team will contain people with a range of perspectives and this can result in additional creativity and synergy of ideas. As the team get to know each other, they will begin to recognize and consider the perspectives of other disciplines. This in turn will help the creative process, generating new ideas through team interaction and collaboration.

Bringing together a group of people to form an effective multidisciplinary team is a challenge. The team needs to be sufficiently diverse with a range of skills balanced for the relevant project and dynamic enough to enable frequent and effective communication.

It is a good approach to build a team at the start of a project so that the team structure can be planned to achieve the specific goals of the project. Even if a particular team member is not required from the outset of the project, it is good to have them recognized as part of the team from the beginning.

If the team is built at the start of a project, it is more likely to be fully informed and committed all the way through to completion. The structure of the team will depend on various factors, including the people available, the goals of the project, the budget and the time scale.

Figure 9
The standard ISO 9241-210 lists ten skill areas for a human-centred design and development team. This chart attempts to match some of the more common skills with a corresponding main skill area from the list. When building a team it is important to decide what each member's job title is, because these are labels that allow others to instantly relate what they do to what they think you do. The process of working towards a common goal of creating an excellent user experience helps a multidisciplinary team to work together.

⊙ uxto.me/f9

Skill Areas, People and Job Titles

ISO Description	People	Typical Title
Application domain expertise, subject matter expertise	People who understand the context of the proposed project, such as a finance expert, football fan or health professional.	
Users and other stakeholder groups (or those that can represent their perspectives)	People who may be affected by the project and people who have the power to affect the project such as regulatory bodies and employees.	
Human factors and ergonomics, usability, accessibility, human–computer interaction, user research	People with specific training in these skills supported by researchers who can deliver insights into the user experience.	
User interface, visual and product design	People with specific training in these skills and probably others including media production, graphic design, illustration and copywriting.	
Systems engineering, hardware and software engineering, programming, production, manufacturing and maintenance	People with technical training in these skills together with a team work ethic and an understanding of a UX Design approach to development.	
Technical writing, training, user support	People with specific training in these skills together with an understanding of the needs of users and stakeholder groups.	

Larger organisations may also include people with these skills

Marketing, branding, sales, technical support and maintenance, health and safety	Human resources, sustainability and other stakeholders
Business analysis, systems analysis	User management, service management and corporate governance

Title Key

R Researcher   E Expert/Author   A Interaction Architect

C Coder   O Product Owner   D User Interface Designer

Methods and background

More than 100 years ago, Henry Ford is reported to have said that if he asked customers what they wanted they would have replied 'faster horses'. This quotation is sometimes used by those who question the idea of centring the design process on the user. When leaps in technology come along, such as the invention of the motor car and the production line, a 'user' is not in a position to conceive the potential impact on their experience. It is argued that users are inherently conservative and will often prefer a familiar design to a new and improved one.

History is peppered with attempts to formalize ways to find out what users want and to create a formula that guarantees success. UX Design is fundamentally a UCD (User Centred Design) approach that also considers the user experience in a particular situation. This is called 'the context of use'.

Instead of asking what users want, we observe what their experience is and think of ways to improve it by using knowledge and skill. So, in the Henry Ford example, we would recognize that faster and more flexible transportation was technically possible and we would work with users to see how this development could improve a range of experiences in their daily lives.

Alternatives to UX Design range from Evolutionary Design, in which case we really would be trying to breed faster horses, to Expert Review, where knowledgeable people decide what is best for us all.

Task Modelling is a method used to analyse the tasks that a user needs to complete in order to reach a goal. The context of the task and the wider user experience is not considered.

Agile, as the name suggests, promotes a fast and flexible approach to development. Key features of an Agile approach include team adaptability to changes in design direction and a willingness by developers to deliver, review and improve designs continually in an iterative cycle.

Usability testing is a method used to assess the quality of an interactive design. There are five components of a usability test: learnability, efficiency, memorability, errors and satisfaction. Usability testing can be used to discover what needs improving in a design, to inform the development process or to validate the product when complete.

These are just a few examples of a wide range of methods that seek to improve the design process and the products of design. Success is measured by their ability to create products that meet design objectives for functionality and performance. They do not generally consider how the product will fit into users' lives or the complicated interplay of factors that lead to providing a good user experience. Often there is no further consideration of the design once the product is released into the wild. A UX Design approach takes a higher-level view. Where any valid method can be shown to provide benefits in improving the user experience then it will be adopted and sometimes adapted to support the design process.

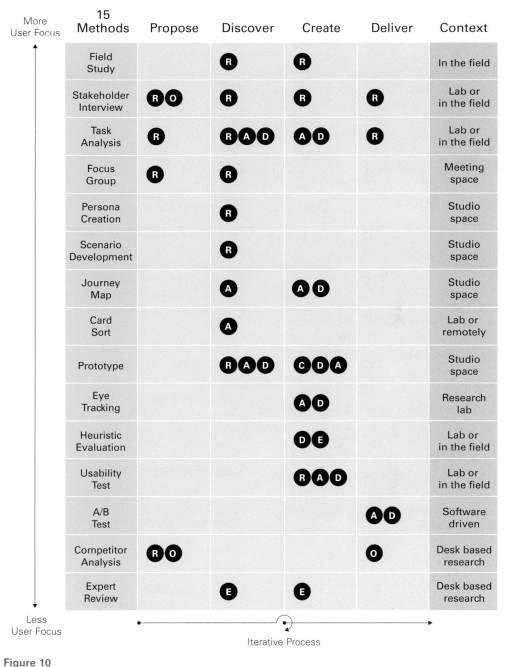

More User Focus ↑ / 15 Methods	Propose	Discover	Create	Deliver	Context
Field Study		R	R		In the field
Stakeholder Interview	R O	R	R	R	Lab or in the field
Task Analysis	R	R A D	A D	R	Lab or in the field
Focus Group	R	R			Meeting space
Persona Creation		R			Studio space
Scenario Development		R			Studio space
Journey Map		A	A D		Studio space
Card Sort		A			Lab or remotely
Prototype		R A D	C D A		Studio space
Eye Tracking			A D		Research lab
Heuristic Evaluation			D E		Lab or in the field
Usability Test			R A D		Lab or in the field
A/B Test				A D	Software driven
Competitor Analysis	R O			O	Desk based research
Expert Review		E	E		Desk based research

Less User Focus ↓

Iterative Process

Figure 10
A table of fifteen common methods used by teams taking a UX Design approach. The methods are ranked by their focus on user experience, when in a typical project they are likely to be applied and who may be expected to apply them. The key to the Role Titles can be found on page 11.

Stakeholders

In every project there are stakeholders. It is obvious that the client has a big stake, and so do their employees and their customers. The design team has a stake because a successful project should pay the bills and salaries, provide job satisfaction and win awards. These are all key stakeholders, but there are likely to be others who should also be considered if the project is to be a success.

Stakeholders who will be affected by a project are said to have an interest in a project. Conversely, stakeholders who can affect a project are said to have power over a project. It is bad news when a stakeholder is not identified until it is too late. It means that the project has not considered their interest or power, and that may cause the project to fail in some way or, worse still, break a regulation or the law.

As part of the project management process a UX Design team will need to:

- Identify all the stakeholders
- Rank them according to their importance in making the project a success
- Develop strategies for understanding their requirements
- Communicate with them and gain their involvement if necessary
- Manage their expectations and keep them happy

One way to identify and rank the priority of stakeholders is to bring the team together to build an influence/interest grid. Team members add sticky notes to the grid, identifying as many stakeholders as possible. Pink notes are used for uninterested or non-supportive stakeholders, and green for those who are supportive. Each note is then placed on the grid in a position relative to the influence and interest of the named stakeholder. This technique helps to visualize the stakeholder 'body' and serves as a reminder to keep the most influential and interested involved in developments.

Activity #2

Designing for others

It is natural for designers to resist the constraints imposed on their creativity when designing for others. Even when the needs of users are carefully considered, the designer must also take account of the context in which the design will be used. This activity introduces the idea of an iterative process of design that focuses on a specific user group and context.

It is best run with small teams of three to four. Each team will need some sticky notes, a timekeeper and someone nominated to write things down.

Follow each step in the sequence and resist the temptation to read ahead if you can. The topic of this exercise is a food menu. Remember, it is the process that we are interested in rather than the topic!

Steps

1 – quick solution
Work as a group to create a single three-course menu that every member of the team agrees would provide them with a great dining experience. Write each course on a separate sticky note and put all three in sequence on a suitable surface.

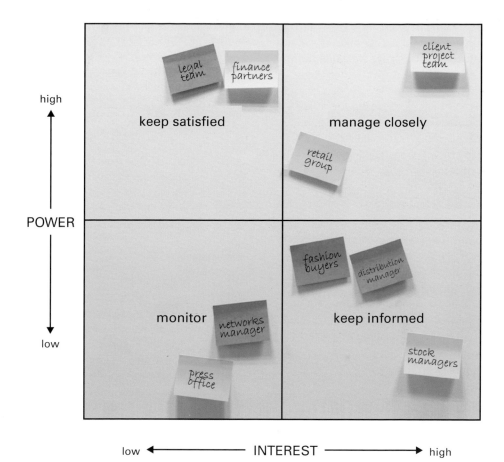

Figure 11
An influence/interest grid representing stakeholders in a project to deliver an online store for a fashion retailer. Easy to update, this simple device can help to keep the project team mindful of the impact of their project in a wider context.
⊙ uxto.me/f11

2 – the user

Having arrived at a suitable menu as a team, you now need to consider if it is suitable for a specific user group. Write each user group listed below on a piece of paper and select one at random.

six-year-old boys

vegetarians

honeymoon couples

fashion models

Discuss the characteristics of the user group and make changes to any of the courses in the existing menu if doing so would provide a better user experience for them. Don't discard the original sticky note, just place any design revisions above it. Aim to make as few changes as possible.

3 – the context

Now that you have a suitable menu for your users, you need to consider the context in which it will be prepared and consumed. Write each context listed below on a piece of paper and select one at random.

 - a street cafe at 1 p.m. on Sunday
 - on holiday in a tent pitched in a field in Ireland with six other people
 - a business class seat on an aircraft flying to Paris
 - a hospital bed in a war zone

Discuss how the characteristics of the context will affect the user. Make changes to any of the courses in the existing menu if doing so would provide a better user experience for the user in the specific context. Again, keep the previous sticky note and place any design revisions above it. Aim to make as few changes as possible.

4 – analysis and review

You may have found that getting everyone in your team to agree on a single menu was difficult and perhaps compromises were needed to reach agreement. If this exercise was run before lunch, then perhaps the 'great dining experience' may have been translated to 'something to satisfy my immediate hunger'.

How did your team relate to the user group chosen at random? Were generalizations and stereotypes evident,

e.g. all small boys like chips or all fashion models eat green salad? Is this sensible and, if not, then how do designers 'connect' with their users?

Did the context make a difference? Should the context be considered earlier in the process? How can a user experience designer control the context in which their work is received? Does the final menu still meet the requirements of Step 1? Have the changes that were made for the defined user and context made the menu unsuitable for all other users?

Outcomes

If the activity has been successful, you should by now begin to understand that the user and context are very important in creating a good user experience. You may have also found that introducing constraints to the design can actually be beneficial in clarifying the scope and providing a sharper focus for the design team. You may be surprised to find that the resulting design may be better at providing a good experience for more of the user groups than the initial design created at Step 1. You could test this by considering the final design against the other user groups and contexts listed.

◉ uxto.me/a2

Figure 12
These four images, loaded with commonly understood cultural and contextual associations, remind us of the need to know more about our users and to consider their context.

Figure 13
UX Designers think sensitively about who the user may be and consider their context. The second activity in this book shows that the use of general or stereotypical models of users can result in designs that fail.

2

Users

In this chapter, we explain how information about users can help you create designs that deliver a better experience. This is easier said than done because it is often unclear who will use a design, where they will use it and why they will use it. There is much less certainty about the user's motivations, expectations and experience when encountering a new interactive design.

The user's world is dynamic and complex and to understand it requires knowledge of user behaviour and the strategic use of research and development methods that are most likely to result in satisfying their expectations.

User research

A UX Design approach requires that potential users are considered early in the development of a project, throughout the project, prior to delivery and continually once the project is in active service. The rewards are tangible, including better performing designs and happier users.

Of course, it is possible to undertake projects without any user research. In such cases, the design will probably be shaped by the design team and their desire to satisfy the funders of the project and their stakeholders. Experience tells us that this approach is unlikely to deliver satisfactory results. It is users who ultimately determine the success or failure of a product or service and so it makes sense to try and understand what it is that they need.

As companies look to interactive media across digital platforms to engage their customers, the consequences of ignoring users in a design and development process can have negative impacts on a company's reputation, brand, operational effectiveness and financial stability.

User research is best started at the beginning of a project because it may be too late to do user research halfway through. By that time any changes may be too fundamental and too costly to implement. Projects can get trapped in a run of cumulative design decisions that make the end product less effective or even completely unusable. Good user research informs the design process, taking away much of the guesswork and providing confidence that the work being done will deliver benefits to the users and the client. Designers who can demonstrate an effective UX Design

approach are in a much better position to ask clients for a budget for user research. Clients are happier to fund user research once they understand the link between what they see as a non-productive phase of the process and the effectiveness of the final product. User research can deliver side-benefits for clients. In some cases, research data about users could potentially be useful in other areas, such as marketing and future product development. Including someone from the client's business within the UX team can help communicate the benefits and outcome of research activities to the rest of their company.

A list of requirements developed through good user research is a sensible starting point when considering the scope and functionality of a new system – although it will not in itself produce a plan for designers to follow. More work will be needed to interpret research results and other factors, such as the availability of new technologies, will influence final design decisions. Two basic questions to ask at the beginning of a new interactive design project are:

(Q1) Who will use it?
(Q2) Why will they use it?

There are a wide range of research methods available to help answer these questions. The answers need to be specific, supported by evidence and detailed.

Demographic descriptors can be used to narrow the answer to Q1 from 'everyone' to a more specific group of potential users. Later in the process it will be beneficial to review individuals from within this group and consider their needs in more detail.

Thinking about demographic groups and individual users provides a focus for the development team. The objective is to achieve a good user experience for this subset of users. This is a pragmatic method to design that overcomes the difficulty of working with large amounts of research. There is likely to be sufficient similarity between the subset and the wider group of target users. The method works because the principal elements of the design will be founded on good research. Like the Menu activity in Chapter 1, there will be a spread of users beyond the target group who achieve a good user experience. This approach is generally considered more successful than attempting to design for every potential user.

Typical demographic descriptors are:

Age range

Ethnicity

Experience

Gender

Income level

Language

Level of educational attainment

Location

Occupation or profession

To answer Q2 it is necessary to identify the user's goal to find the reason 'why'. The example below extracts the main goal and a number of user requirements from a specific question about navigation.

Q: Why would you use a sat-nav application?

A: To be guided to an unfamiliar location

Goal: To arrive at the correct location

Requirements:

To identify the most efficient route

To receive clear directions

To be updated on journey progress, location and estimated arrival time

In UX Design the question "Why would you use a sat-nav application" could be considered too specific. A more open question could identify the group that the designers are targeting more reliably. Alternatively, it could reveal why some groups do not use sat-nav. Here is an example of a more open question.

Q: How do you find your way around when driving around the country?

A1: I use an in car sat-nav

A2: I use a map and follow road signs

A3: My passengers tell me the way

Clearly this question could be answered in many different ways, but the goal and the requirements are likely to be very similar. Have a go at the activity later in this chapter to practice asking the right questions, discovering real goals and identifying requirements. This groundwork at the research stage of UX Design helps to ensure that initial designs are on the right track.

The user's world

In addition to the 'who?' and 'why?' questions there is another question that needs to be asked. It's the obvious and yet often overlooked question – where?

The UX Design term for the situation in which users will use an interactive design is the 'context of use'. The context can encompass the physical location, the current activity or inactivity of the user, or the user's interaction with other systems, people and their environment. Your design should recognize the context in which it will be used and be sympathetic to the user's situation.

There are a number of ways to find out about the user's world. Some involve asking questions such as 'how far do you travel to work each day?' which would provide quantitative data. This can be used to find information such as the average journey distance, time taken and so on.

Questions for which the answers are not quantities, such as 'do you feel lonely on your daily commute?' reveal qualitative data and can provide deeper insights into the experience of the individual. Qualitative data is less easy to process into the reliable information needed to inform the design process. Getting the questions right and interpreting the data correctly is a highly skilled job.

Questioning people is a relatively cheap and simple method to find out about the users' world. Other methods of research include interviews, focus groups and field studies.

Interviews and focus groups

One-to-one interviews help the design team to understand a sample of individuals in more detail. Focus groups will typically involve talking to five or more users at once. The advantage here is that the dynamics within the group may bring up topics for discussion that would not arise in an interview situation.

Field studies

The purpose of observing users in the 'field' (the term 'ethnography' is sometimes borrowed from social sciences to describe this idea) is to challenge any assumptions that the designer may already have about the user group and their context. Field studies can provide abundant data, so it is a good idea to record as much as possible (ideally with video) so that user behaviour can be carefully examined later on.

Generative approaches

A more creative method is to ask each user to generate research material, such as a diary. Written or audio/visual diaries allow users to document their daily activity. Designers can use these artefacts to probe feelings about relevant experiences.

Figure 14
The Third Wave Kiosk in Torquay, Australia, was built by Tony Hobba Architects from materials typically used for the construction of seawalls or piers. The surface, form and colours of the kiosk are sensitive to the surroundings, its rusty hues and undulating folds matching the tones and shapes of the nearby cliffs. The kiosk also influences the behaviour of visitors to the beach, providing a distinct meeting point, as well as changing rooms, toilets, and a cafe.

Co-experience

Because we are social creatures, many of our experiences involve other people. Networked games and social websites clearly have a social purpose, but virtually all other experiences have a shared dimension: printing holiday snaps, booking a hotel, renewing your travel insurance, watching a video, ordering a meal; all of these may involve interaction with friends, colleagues, family-members, experts, or strangers. The way we act with our families is different to the way we act with our friends. The way that we act with authority figures, such as a teacher, boss or doctor, is not the same way we act in the company of strangers. The important thing to recognize is that it is all an act: in different social situations, we perform a social role that is appropriate to the setting, and the people around us are an audience. Typically, we show mutual respect for each other's social roles by using strategies such as cooperation, politeness, praise and deference.

Rewarding co-experiences are ones that provide channels for this exchange of goodwill. Even when experiences are solitary, they are the currency of social interaction. We talk about things we have done, things we have enjoyed – even negative experiences can yield amusing anecdotes. When we talk about user context, we should consider more than the ergonomics of the spatial environment. We must also think about the social dimension of an experience, intended or not, and consider how that will affect our emotional response to the experience.

Figure 15
Moving images interplay with surfaces of buildings in a projection. Events like this are designed to be experienced by groups and individuals in public settings, but all experiences, even solitary ones, have the potential to live on in social media settings as users discuss, share and tweet their experiences.

Activity #3

Listening and learning

This activity challenges you to break out of the designer bubble and talk to other humans. People you expect to use whatever you plan to create. Maybe not the actual intended users, but a range of people who are at least representative of them. You will need to take an open and careful approach to discussion together with keen listening skills. The aim of this research is to clarify ideas so that the design process moves in the right direction. Initial conversations with potential users can provide a good foundation for wider research using other methods.

Proposal

You may already have a potential app design to discuss. Alternatively, here is an idea to get you started:

An existing soft drink company is planning to create a smartphone app that guides customers to their nearest vending machine so that they can purchase from an exclusive range of drinks and snacks. Proposed features for the app include remote viewing of product availability, remote vending, payment by smartphone and the facility for customers to provide feedback to the company.

Steps

1 – user characteristics

Your first task is to find people who are likely to use the app. Write a short description of their characteristics and use it to select potential participants for discussion.

2 – environment

Identify a place where you can find participants and write yourself a short script that introduces you and the purpose of your enquiries. A good place could be in the vicinity of a vending machine.

3 – engagement

Without asking direct questions, chat about the app idea with at least five people in individual face-to-face discussions. Be alert to clues about their routines and what they think about the idea. Be neutral when you present the scenario, perhaps by saying "I have been asked to talk with you about an idea for a new smartphone app" rather than "My team are designing a new smartphone app and we would like to hear what you think of our idea". The latter would indicate that you are personally invested in the idea and the interviewee may then be guarded about making any negative comments. Assure participants that their responses are anonymous. Be careful to avoid straying into topics that are personal or irrelevant to your research.

4 – findings

After each conversation make notes to record what the participant had to say. Try not to structure responses as answers to questions. At this stage you are looking to discover sentiment, suggestions and to reveal potential problems. If the idea is received positively then the team can move forward with some confidence. Alternatively, negative sentiments may suggest flaws in the idea. In either case the benefits of early research are clear. As a bonus, because the style of this research was discussion rather than questioning, participants may have contributed new ideas and solutions for the design team to consider.

Talking with potential users from the very start of a new project is a surprisingly simple way to expand the thinking and horizons of a UX Team.

◉ uxto.me/a3

Figure 16
There's a world outside the studio.

Emotional responses

Experiences can feel good, or they can feel bad. It is difficult to predict exactly what emotions an experience might provoke. But it is possible to understand some of the factors that influence our emotional responses, and the way that these can enhance or undermine an experience.

The function of a movie is to tell a story, which requires strong characters and an intriguing plot. This is why a 90-minute compilation of chase sequences would not produce a positive behavioural response in the audience, even though the spectacle may produce a viscerally satisfying hour-and-a-half.

In his book Emotional Design (2005), Donald Norman categorizes three types of responses to designed products or experiences. He calls these responses visceral, behavioural and reflective.

A reflective response is one that activates our critical faculties. We evaluate and judge experiences against personal values, such as pride, cynicism, loyalty and self-image. Our enduring memories of an experience arise from reflections like this, and these may influence our future use of products or services.

Visceral, behavioural and reflective responses

Our initial 'gut' reaction is our visceral response; one which involves base instincts, such as fear, desire, attraction, repulsion, or shock. For example, the thrill of riding a roller coaster is a typically visceral experience. Similarly, a sleek, weighty, smartphone may induce a visceral reaction just by holding it and gazing at its contours.

Behavioural responses consider function: how fully or easily something does the thing it is designed to do. Negative behavioural responses arise if an experience is frustrating or confusing. Positive behavioural responses arise from good ergonomics and good interaction design.

At a reflective level, we may admire the elegance or cleverness of a design solution. We may be equally conscious of how others may perceive us as consumers or participants.

Peer pressure may influence a user's reflective judgment, regardless of behavioural considerations such as usability or affordability, so it is worth observing the social dimension of user experience in your target users and in the development of your designs.

Figure 17
For designer Jordi Parra, the idea of 'music as a gift' was an important emotional element of the concept behind the Spotify Box. The tokens represent different music play-lists; the proximity of the tokens alerts the box to play the appropriate tracks via the music-sharing platform. The discs provide a tactile, visceral pleasure to the experience of digital music, as well as the reflective, social experience of collecting and sharing.

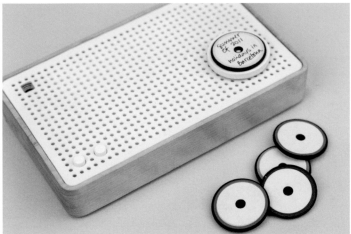

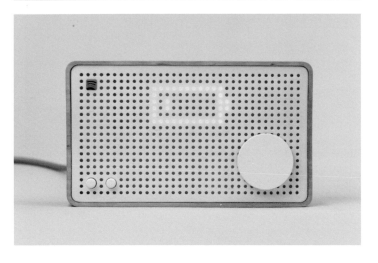

Memory

Experiences are often sequential within a timespan, requiring the participant to retain key information from step to step. However, the capacity of most people to remember things is limited. Designers can ease the mental load on the user by creating experiences that require understanding and recognition rather than recollection.

Usability guru Jakob Nielsen believes that minimizing memory-load is one of the most important features of a user interface design. Users should never have to remember something, or retrace their steps, in order to make sense of what is in front of them.

Short-term versus long-term memory

Our short-term memory is little more than a temporary buffer for holding pertinent information. It is volatile, and only by a process of mental encoding can this information be stored more permanently in our long-term memory. In order for our long-term memory to be engaged, our minds must use a process of association and organization to enable the memories to 'stick'. The name for this personal model of organizing information and experience in the mind is a 'schema'.

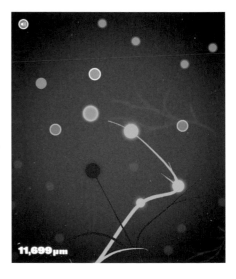

Mnemonics

Most schemata are personally constructed and based upon previous experiences. A mnemonic is a schema that is designed by one person for somebody else to use. The single-sentenced fable 'Richard Of York Gave Battle In Vain' is a familiar mnemonic that encodes the sequence of colours of the rainbow; the initial letters match the first letters of the colour sequence red, orange, yellow, green, blue, indigo and violet. Mnemonics, like mental 'zip files', can be useful ways to compress otherwise cryptic information, such as passwords. Musical melodies and jingles can act as mnemonics, helping us to store important phrases or number sequences.

Metaphors

A metaphor is a way of comparing an unfamiliar concept or situation to a familiar one. The computer desktop is a metaphor relating the (initially) new experience of navigating a computer system to the familiar rules of an office workspace. New platforms and experiences will require sensibly constructed metaphors so that users can migrate from the known to the unknown. Metaphors allow the user to apply what they already know, which is easier than memorizing something new.

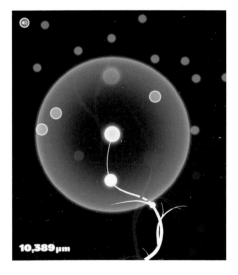

Figure 18
In Axon, created for the Wellcome Trust by Preloaded, the player takes on the viewpoint of a neuron inside the brain. The goal of the game is to form long neuron connections by clicking on protein 'targets' within the active circle of influence. The interface of the game is elegantly simple, thus avoiding information overload. The behaviour of 'special' targets, which may accelerate the growth, or increase the circle of influence, is learned as they are encountered. The user has no need to load their memory with complex rules and abstract controls – they just play.

Fallibility

When things go wrong and negative experiences are created, it is tempting to blame the people involved rather than the design. But errors are more often the result of a design that misleads, confuses or distracts the people who use it.

Fallibility experts have defined several types of error. A 'slip' occurs when the user plans to act correctly, but inadvertently performs an incorrect action. Slips may be spotted if appropriate feedback mechanisms keep users informed of their actions. The impact of slips can be reduced if the users have the scope to 'undo' their actions.

'Lapses' occur when too many demands are placed on our attention or memory; we plan a correct action but forget to execute it. Lapses can be minimized by use of simplicity and consistency in the visual design's hierarchy and emphasis. For example, by including progress indicators and validation procedures that lessen the cognitive load on the user.

A 'mistake' occurs when an incorrect action is planned and faithfully executed. It would be unfair to blame people for mistakes made as a result of unrealistic expectations held by the designer. For example, when users have been conditioned to act one way, and are suddenly required to break a familiar pattern.

A more wilful error is a 'violation', seen when someone intentionally breaks the rules of a system. A degree of behaviour control is required to avert violations. Careful observation of the users and their contexts may help to better understand their expectations and motivations, and to give some explanation for their actions.

In some European cities, the 'Don't Walk' symbol on pedestrian crossings is supplemented by countdown timers to indicate the remaining time until the safe crossing interval. The timers may seem redundant, as the lights change very frequently, and the crossing light symbols are universally understood. It seems that people are less stressed when they know how long they need to wait. The countdown encourages them not to make opportunistic attempts to cross the road and risk a serious accident.

As the architects of positive experiences, designers should respect that we can all be less than perfect. When things go wrong, the user should be alerted without criticism or condescension. Everybody is fallible, but there are few things more likely to create a negative user experience than being made to feel like a failure.

Figure 19
We all like to know how long we may need to wait at a junction but for cyclists the temptation to ignore a stop signal is a potentially fatal violation. This cycle lane signal in Amsterdam counts down the seconds until the lights change in favour of the cyclist. The creators know through statistical data analysis that their design will help prevent injury and loss of life.

Expectation

Philosopher Immanuel Kant claimed that a sense of cause and effect is innate; that is, we are born with an expectation that every action has some kind of consequence. Our memories of causes and effects are amassed into a model of the world that shapes our expectations of all future experiences. In general, negative experiences result when reality does not match our mental model of how things respond and develop.

Feedback

We may not expect a kettle to boil water instantaneously, but we do expect immediate confirmation that the 'on' button has been activated. Feedback is a way of acknowledging that an action like this has occurred.

Audible feedback may be a mere beep. Visual feedback may be a subtle state-change of a user interface. Feedback can be tactile too: the reassuring 'clunk' of a switch provides feedback that the switching action has been registered.

Closure

One of the most comforting expectations that a user will have is a demand for closure or 'resolution' to denote that the experience is at an end. When a movie ends, the credits roll and the closing music plays; in an online transaction, final confirmation and payment must be acknowledged and confirmed, and delivery information announced. Without clear closure, a user will be left hanging, asking themselves, 'Are we done . . .?'

Consistency

Users will reasonably expect similar things to behave in a similar way. Consider the game universe of a first-person shooter game: some doors may be opened and explored, whereas others, due to the boundaries of the game world, are merely surface decoration. There must be a distinct visual difference to these different doors to denote their contrasting behaviour, otherwise the logic of the game world will appear to break down. The same principle can be applied to all types of interfaces and controls.

Confounding expectations

Users may get frustrated if events are not what they expect. However, confounding expectations is not always a bad thing. If the outcome is different to what is expected, but still satisfying, then the result is pleasant surprise; whereas suspense can be created by delaying or withholding an outcome.

Figure 20
Michael Hansen created this record sleeve for the music of modern classical composer Allan Gravgaard Madsen. The intricate print design also appears on the surface of the vinyl revealing a kaleidoscope dance of crystalline shapes and patterns when played on a turntable under a strobe light. The record and packaging provide an unconventional and unexpected dimension to the experience of playing a record, listening to music or reading cover notes.

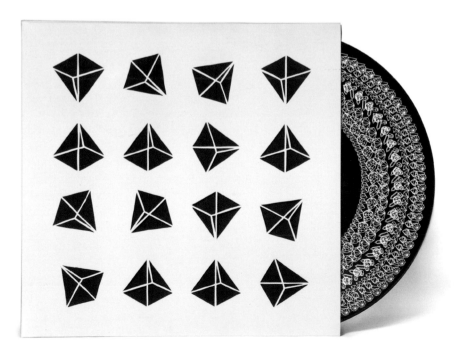

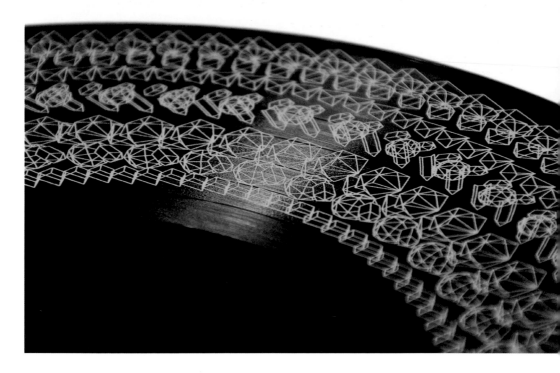

50 Hz STROBE
LIGHT ANIMATION

Motivation

Motivation is the influence of inner desires on outward behaviour. Most human behaviour can be attributed to several basic desires or needs, and this can explain what drives people to participate in a sustained experience.

All human beings need acceptance from a peer group, and this requirement can influence our behaviour. In addition, human beings have an underlying appetite to have influence over others, to have status within their own peer group, and to exercise power or vengeance over opposing groups. This may manifest itself as competitive urges in games or status in peer-review forums.

Once status within a group has been achieved, the need to become more individual arises. There may be an appetite for learning for its own sake, or the desire to have an influence over the environment, by organizing or by possessing things. Equally, altruistic forces may take prominence, such as gaining satisfaction from helping others.

The most fundamental human needs are the requirements for food, exercise and safety. If safety is violated, then all other motivating forces vanish. Users must have confidence in the security of their experience; otherwise they will feel fear or anxiety. It is important that experiences should promote a feeling of security and trust, especially if the task relies upon extrinsic motivation.

Extrinsic versus intrinsic motivation

Some experiences contain the rewards for participation, so these are described as intrinsically motivated and the motivation comes from within. Playing games is usually intrinsically motivated, as achievement or progress within the game provides its own rewards. In contrast, completing a tax return is unlikely be intrinsically motivating. In this case, extrinsic (external) forces provide the motivation, such as the fear of penalties or a sense of duty. Similarly, the task of designing a bespoke business card at a self-printing kiosk may be externally motivated by the desire for prestige or status.

In all cases, it is a good idea to consider exactly what will energize a user to perform a task, or to sustain an experience. Designers can incorporate reminders of what is at stake. Progress bars, leader boards, rewards and even appropriate imagery can all reinforce motivated behaviour.

The action of writing a customer review for goods or services may be motivated by a selfish appetite for status or achievement points, but it can also be motivated by a selfless desire to share information and care for others.

Figure 21
Duolingo is a free language learning app which motivates learners in a variety of ingenious ways: bite-sized lessons resemble games, so that points are earned for completing lessons; virtual currency can be earned and exchanged for additional lives, and commitment to ongoing learning is encouraged by seeing how many days in a row are spent learning a language.

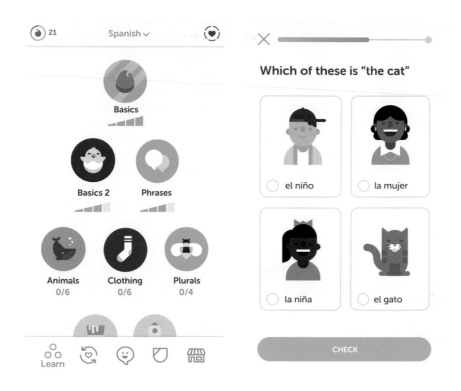

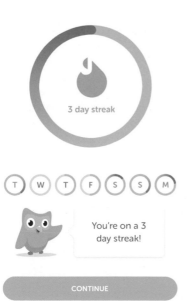

Activity #4

The journey concept

Interactive media offers a form of experience in which the user has some control over the system they are using.

Often this control involves navigating through content and making choices in order to achieve a goal, such as sending a message or paying for items purchased. The user's progress towards their goal in an interactive system can be thought of as a journey.

A 'user journey' is analogous to one in the physical world, having a starting point and multiple potential routes. Similarly, it is possible to get lost in an interactive system, take a wrong direction or get completely stuck. Unlike a real journey a user can abandon an interactive journey at any point. This can have consequences for applications and websites that rely on their users to complete tasks, such as completing a payment process, and so designers usually need to make a user's journey as smooth as possible.

There are at least three user journey methods in a UX Design approach that can be applied to help improve an interactive design:

Designers can ask users to envisage a journey to help shape an early navigational design.

Insights can be derived by observing users making journeys through prototypes of the design.

Designs can be analysed to reveal data about actual user journeys once they are up and running. This live analysis is done by tracking user interactions.

In this activity you will try out methods one and two, envisaging and observing, with the aim of improving the user experience in a small-scale interactive design. Using these methods should minimize any serious problems with user navigation before the design is implemented. Method three, live analysis, allows designers to optimize the user experience based on large amounts of data over significant time periods. It is not possible to use method three without deploying the design, but it is worth noting its existence here because it has the potential to validate the work done through envisaging and observing.

Activity requirements

You will need pencil and paper and one or more people to provide their ideas and feedback. For the optional step 4 you will also need access to a computer and basic prototyping software.

Steps

1 – create a scenario

If you are working on a project, then create a scenario in which a user will use your design to complete a task and achieve a goal. Alternatively create a scenario for an imagined system, for example: 'Thirteen-year-old Gemma is taking part in a nature study and needs help to identify wild birds in her garden. Count the number of times she sees them in an hour and submit the information to a wildlife charity.'

2 – ask the user to envisage the journey

Explain the scenario and ask the user to describe how they will approach the task. Depending on the user they may prefer to explain how they would achieve the task in the absence of a fully interactive system. In Gemma's case she may refer to illustrations in a printed guide to identify different wild birds, use a note pad to record when she sees a particular type of bird and submit her research to the website by using an online form. As someone interested in UX Design you probably already see the potential for interactive media to improve the user experience for Gemma. For the purpose of this activity the last stage of the task, entering data to the website form, will provide a sufficient challenge to recognize the benefits of creating a user journey.

Encourage the user to think freely, without constraints imposed by screens or website pages. Make lots of notes to use in the next step.

3 – visualize the journey

Using pencil and paper, turn the user's ideas of the journey into a sequence of sketched frames. For Gemma's journey, from paper notepad to entering data using a web form, visualize each step in the route, identifying points at which Gemma can make a choice of direction and show these as branches from the main route.

See if you can identify 'break points' where Gemma may take a wrong turn, get stuck or just irritated with the process. Carefully consider what changes could be made to improve the experience. Look for ways to remove the need for the user to repeat tasks such as re-entering data or looping through multiple steps that could be achieved in one stage.

4 – make the journey (optional)

You may like to create a mock-up of the design using a quick prototype. There are many tools that can link sketch designs by making images (or parts of images) clickable. See Chapter 6.

5 – observe users making the journey

Sit with one or more users and ask them to make the journey using the sequence of sketched frames or quick prototype as a visual aid. Keep a focus on the original scenario and remind users of their task and goal. Be alert to inevitable user comments such as 'how do I do that?' and 'where do I go now?' Answer such questions with 'how would you like to do that?' or 'where do you need to go?' The activity will be revealing and should result in many suggested changes to the original design. These suggestions need to be recorded so that they are not missed when developing the second iteration of the design.

◉ uxto.me/a4

Outcomes

If this activity has been successful then you will have revealed differences between your initial concept of the user journey, the user's envisaged journey and the observed journey. It is likely that you will have identified 'break points' with the potential to alienate the user through poor interaction design. You should recognize that, for relatively little effort, these methods can dramatically improve the user experience when used to help shape interaction designs. They also reduce the risk of poor or failing designs finding their way into the real world and act as insurance against live analysis proving that the initial designs were defective.

Gemma's BGB User Journey

...followed a link to the RSPB website

I discovered the BGB!
on Facebook,
from my teacher
and on dad's car radio.

...read instructions!
register online
wait for pack to arrive

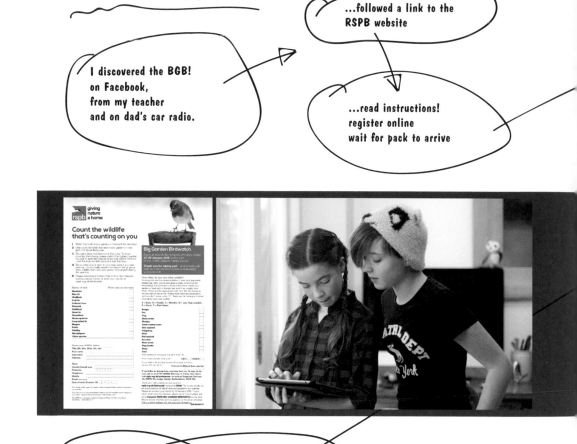

...will I be able to identify the birds? Dad showed me an iPad app that could help.

...doing some practice birdwatching before school every day! So far I have spotted 7 different birds but I'm not sure what they are called.

Figure 22
Visualizing Gemma's journey through the RSPB Big Garden Birdwatch.

...the pack arrived!
read instructions again!
BGB is on the last
weekend in January.
Mum chooses Sunday.

...my friend Nathalie
is coming to help.

...we're borrowing my grandad's
binoculars.

...it's the big day.
We saw lots of birds in the garden.
Sometimes it was difficult to agree
on the type of bird we saw.

...mum completed the paper form and
sent it back to the RSPB. I put some photos on Facebook
for my friends to see. I think we'll do the BGB again
next year!

3

Experience design

Creating a good user experience requires knowledge of the subjective human factors that define them. When users describe an interface as intuitive or fun, they are doing so in the context of their own situation and life experience. In this chapter, we discuss some of the more common user factors, explain how an understanding of them can inform the decisions that shape a new interactive design, and show how this approach is needed to achieve other benefits, such as competitive advantage and productivity.

Competitive advantage

Competitive advantage is a term used to describe the characteristics of a product or service that makes it more likely to be successful than others in the same market. The factors that give products and services competitive advantage include price, availability, design and functionality. In a market where there is strong competition, products that have been around for a while reach a point where maintaining competitive advantage can be difficult. One way to gain new competitive advantage is to learn more about the user experience through user research. Good research will reveal insights into users' attitudes and show where the product fits in to their daily lives. It will provide a strong basis on which to refine the existing product and reveal any potential for similar or new products. User-centred product improvement is the most effective way to fend off competition and keep users happy.

There are times when your client may ask you to justify a UX Design approach. You could respond by arguing that designs that deliver a good user experience will be more successful and ultimately more rewarding. In the commercial world you will also need to show how UX Design can create additional competitive advantage, maintaining or growing the client's position in the marketplace.

Explaining the potential benefits of applying a UX Design approach needs to be done on a project by project basis. In some cases, the UX team can quickly see how market share is being lost and deliver quick solutions. Where existing designs are failing for no obvious reason some detective work will be needed with the help of potential and existing users.

Before a new project starts the client could be asked 'How do you think you can make your product or service more competitive?' The client is likely to respond with ideas that are directly related to their perspective on the product or service. They might say that their product should be more visible, more competitively priced, more attractive and include more functionality. If the same question were asked of the users they might say that it should be made more user-friendly, more affordable, easier to use, quicker to use, do more things, do fewer things, work with other products, be more robust and require less thinking. It is the job of a UX Design team to provide solutions to the challenges that are presented by user research.

Within user interface design there can be a tension between commercial interests and the user experience. Dark UX is a term for designs that aim to trick users. The use of Dark UX risks alienating customers for short-term gain. Examples include making it difficult to stop services by styling links in unreadable type or sneakily adding unwanted goods to orders at the checkout stage. Legislators in the European Union have been active in outlawing unethical practice and fining companies who do not comply with the law. This is one area where the UX Design team need to be careful when responding to design requests that conflict with ethical practice.

Figure 23
Matterport's 3D visualization technology creates real-world environments that include hotspots to automatically trigger context-specific video and other content.

Brands

Branding is a marketing tool. In developing a brand, the goal of marketers is to create an attitude in the mind of the consumer towards a product in order to differentiate it from competing goods and services. Branding is a way in which a provider can make a 'promise' to a user, that an experience will deliver recognizable and consistent values. Effective branding can add value to a product or service to the degree that the consumer will pay a premium for that brand.

Companies may reinforce their brand position by sponsoring events that reflect their brand ideals, or by using endorsements from celebrities who typify those ideals. Brand identities are most often upheld by consistently communicating and delivering a user experience that embodies those ideals.

Should the user have any negative experiences associated with the brand,

Figure 24
How do you convey a sense of community before the community exists? This was the challenge for The Neighbourhood, who designed an iconic and evocative brand identity to bring to life the vision of the Middlewood Locks development in Manchester, UK.

then the brand is tainted and can become devalued. What is more, developing and maintaining a brand can be a very expensive investment for a company. For these reasons, most corporations protect and manage their brand identities very carefully.

Brands are the result of a sustained and informed business strategy and do not emerge overnight. You may find yourself in a position where you are producing work that must conform to brand expectations. By developing a good understanding of the brand you will gain insights into the expectations of the end user.

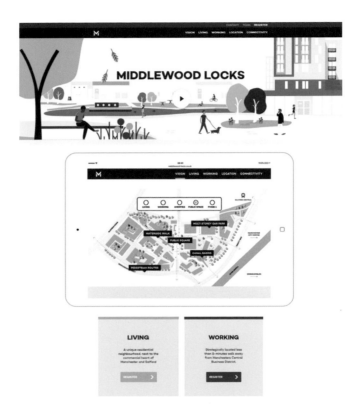

Productivity

In every area of human life there are different ways to approach tasks and achieve objectives. We recognize productivity as a word used to describe the efficiency of a particular approach to a task.

By recording the time taken to complete a task and assessing what has been produced, it is possible to measure levels of productivity. When designing interactive applications, it is useful to consider the user and their need to be productive. It may help to think of the system that you are designing as a tool.

High levels of productivity will be achieved if the tool is well matched both to the user and to the task. Subtle changes in the design can make big changes to levels of productivity, particularly when the system is large scale and involves many users.

The relationship between user satisfaction and productivity is complex and will vary depending on the context of the task and the user.

If it were possible to design away all the challenges of a task, it would be less satisfying to most users. When an interactive design is thought to be difficult to use, or reduces productivity by requiring needless steps, then this is both unsatisfying and unproductive.

Users need well-balanced and flexible designs that allow them to be productive and to gain satisfaction by applying their ability and effort to the best effect.

Figure 25
Preloaded designed this app for the National Museums of Scotland to help young people develop their creative skills. Unique human and animal faces are generated by interchanging different heads, eyes, noses and mouths which can then be printed and worn as a mask or displayed as a poster.

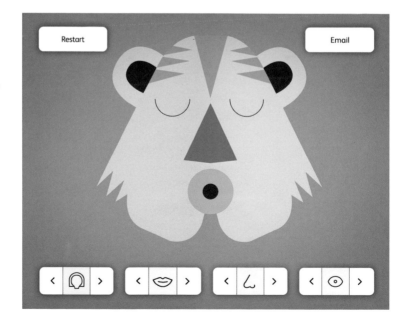

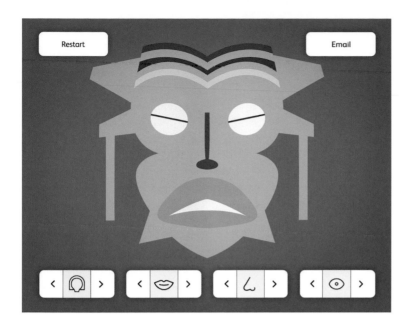

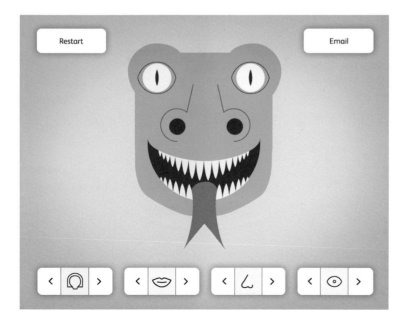

Activity #5

Quantifying sentiment

Our mood can change the way that we feel about our experiences when interacting with technology. Research shows that affective experiences will trigger feelings that cause us to think differently. This is as true when the affect is positive or negative. In this activity you will aim to measure the affect using a scale of positive and negative words in a simple questionnaire.

Steps

1. Make a list of 20 words which describe feelings and emotions. Half of the words should have a positive meaning and the remainder should have a negative meaning.

2. Create a five-column table like the one shown, arranging the positive and negative words in the 'Feeling' column so that the positive feelings are alongside the clear boxes in the first 'Check' column.

3. Cover the 'Check' columns with a piece of paper or cut-out a flap from the sheet and fold over.

4. Think back to circumstances when you used a digital product or service for the first time, perhaps using some unfamiliar technology.

5. Write a score between 1 and 5 in the 'Score' column to best describe your feelings on that occasion using the scale provided, or devise your own scale.

6. Copy the scores to the blank boxes in the 'Check' columns. Add the scores for positive words and subtract the result from the total of the negative words.

Scoring

The result should range between 40 and minus 40. A score of zero indicates that your mood was average or neutral. A score below zero indicates a negative mood, feeling sad and depressed, where –40 is distressing and not at all pleasurable. A score above zero indicates a positive mood, feeling enthusiastic, active and alert, with +40 indicating pleasurable engagement, high energy and full concentration.

Outcome

This activity should have started you thinking about how your designs can affect the mood state of the people who use them. Rather like the writer of a play, you have the ability to craft your work to influence the emotional state of your audience. The PANAS test (Positive and Negative Affect Schedule) is a proven method to estimate the level of affect. It can be applied in user testing to help inform the design process, revealing unintentional negative effects and confirming the positive.

⊙ uxto.me/a4

Figure 26
For this activity we suggested that you could choose your own words and scale in the questions. For the test to be accurate you should probably use the specific words and scale in the original research shown here. Full reference: Watson, D., Clark, L. A., & Tellegan, A. (1988). Development and validation of brief measures of positive and negative affect: The PANAS scales. *Journal of Personality and Social Psychology*, 54(6), 1063–1070.

Scale				
Very slightly or not at all	A little	Moderately	Quite a bit	Extremely
1	2	3	4	5

	Feeling	Score		Check
1	Interested			
2	Distressed			
3	Excited			
4	Upset			
5	Strong			
6	Guilty			
7	Scared			
8	Hostile			
9	Enthusiastic			
10	Proud			
11	Irritable			
12	Alert			
13	Ashamed			
14	Inspired			
15	Nervous			
16	Determined			
17	Attentive			
18	Jittery			
19	Active			
20	Afraid			

fold the flap over the check area when entering scores - copy scores across to the blank check cells when finished

flap

Result

Totals		-	=

Fun

Fun is a difficult concept to define. 'Fun' can have connotations of triviality and frivolity, but fun operates on a much more meaningful level if the goal is to provide true value to users.

Fun usually involves some kind of discovery by recognizing something unusual but reconciling it with our understanding of the rules of a system.

Fun belongs to the part of our nature that desires challenge and growth as well as order and security. Gestalt theory shows us that humans are reassured by patterns. The more we can make sense of things, and organize them, the more secure we feel. But once a pattern is identified, it can become repetitive and boring.

We are naturally inquisitive, and seek out new places, new situations, and new patterns to expand our world view. Interaction is – or should be – intrinsically fun, because interacting with other people or with our environment is the primary way of exploring and discovering.

For a baby, the game of peekaboo is fun. The baby is at a stage of development where a new understanding of object permanence is emerging, and there is joy to be had in learning that things still exist in the world, even when they disappear from view.

For an older child, it may be tremendous fun to press a button for a lift or a pedestrian crossing. The joy of being a cause to an effect is a gratifying system of discovery that gives them a new insight into their place in the world. As we grow older and become more self-aware, we strive to achieve some mastery in controlling our environment, whether this is customizing our Facebook page, climbing a mountain or completing the next level of a computer game.

Mihaly Csikszentmihalyi, an expert in fun and fulfilment, warns against confusing fun with 'leisure'. Leisure describes a type of consumption which may not necessarily be that rewarding. Fun, on the other hand, is driven by personal satisfaction.

The craft of designing 'fun' lies in the ability to balance what is familiar with what is uncertain. Fun is not something that is bolted on to an experience in the form of silly music, cute characters or dazzling visuals. Fun is an integral part of an experience that relies upon understanding the expectations, motivations and abilities of the user.

Figure 27
A charming and award winning concept for packaging for pasta by Nikiita Konkin. The witty visual parallel between hairstyles and pasta shapes creates memorable and stylish containers for varieties of the everyday foodstuff.

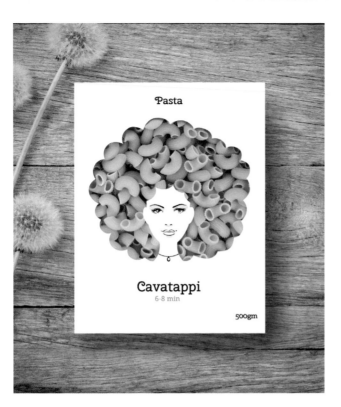

Usability

Usability is a measure of how easily a user can achieve a goal such as entering a building, filling a bathtub with water or ordering a pizza online. It is a subjective measure because levels of usability depend on the user and the context of use. It is also a comparative measure because it aims to compare levels of usability in different designs that attempt to achieve the same goal for users.

Usability testing is carried out to find the functional effectiveness of designs without considering the wider user experience. It is important that designs work for users in a practical and efficient way, but it is also important to recognize that usability methods are just one tool in the design process.

Designers need to balance the user's need for stimulation, challenge, discovery and fun against utility and conformity.

Figure 28
Brave designed the Felix Wellness Platform to help government employees track their fitness and well-being. Recognizing that the typical user has many existing responsibilities, Brave designed the platform to be easy to use, including many ways for users to customize their experience and make sense of data generated from tracking their nutrition, sleep, stress, weight and physical activities.

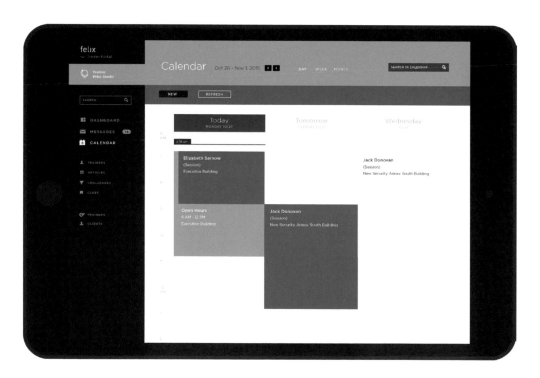

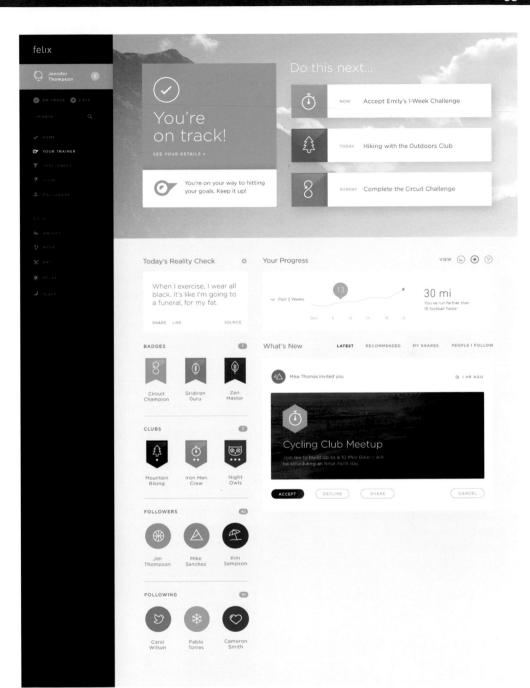

Simplicity

Simplicity is a virtue beloved by designers in all disciplines. When applied sensitively and intelligently, simplicity eases the load on the user's memory and attention.

There are several ways in which experiences can be simplified: context menus are a common way of accessing timely features; a 'recent places' or 'last played' option is sensitive to the user's usual behaviour; geo-location technology has empowered some devices to make assumptions about users' needs and wants. But for some users, these simplifications are presumptions that threaten privacy and undermine an experience.

Advocates of simplicity often mistakenly believe that any feature that does not aid functionality and usability is redundant and should be purged. But we should not mistake the principle of simplicity for a mission of sparse minimalism. Aesthetics have a purpose because they contribute to the overall experience. They may be what makes the difference between a usable experience and an enjoyable one.

It may be more useful to think of simplicity as the intelligent management of complexity. When users demand simplicity, they are really asking for sensitivity to their present goals and needs. Simplicity does not mean reducing opportunities for interactions; it means framing these opportunities within a relevant and consistent schema.

Challenge

Challenge is a highly subjective part of an experience. A colouring book represents a challenge to a child, because their manual dexterity and colour perception is still developing and their chances of success in the endeavour are as likely as failure. Satisfying experiences are those that recognize and accommodate the evolving skills of the user, and in return present them with appropriate and achievable challenges.

Such experiences provide the user with a realistic opportunity for mastery, and this is a highly motivating force.

When the opportunity for mastery is in a perfectly attuned balance with the degree of challenge, then the user may enter a state called 'flow'. A 'flow' state is so absorbing that we lose all sense of time and purpose. The task becomes intrinsically motivating and participation is its own reward. A state of flow can be achieved by reading an absorbing book, by playing a musical instrument, or by engaging in extreme sports.

There are several factors that create the potential for flow. It is important that the goals of the task are clear, but it is also crucial that the user receives feedback to assess how comfortably they are developing the skills required to meet imminent challenges. Games have obvious mechanisms that evolve to challenge the evolving competence of the player. But other experiences can utilize the principles of challenges to engage a user.

Figure 29
The website portfolio of digital studio Rotate° is an elegantly simple design built around restricted tones, subtle textures, and a single, recurring disc. Although their client-based projects and case-studies are often rich in detail and sophistically executed, the key features of each are represented in a series of concise tableaux.

Rotate°
Brand, Design & Build

Menu

Seedlip
A dash of eCommerce excellence
for the world's first distilled non-
alcoholic spirits

& Marketing

SEEDLIP
DISTILLED NON-ALCOHOLIC SPIRITS

Menu

Design, Build, Marketing

Feedback

Learning the piano has the potential for flow, because we receive constant and immediate feedback on our progress: we can hear at once if we have played the correct note at the right moment and can adjust our performance accordingly

if an error is made. Conversely, some experiences do not provide the immediate reassurance that our actions, if not wholly successful, are within a margin of manageable failure. These are the experiences that we abandon out of frustration.

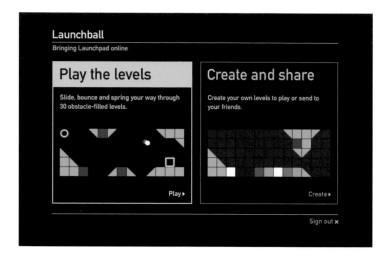

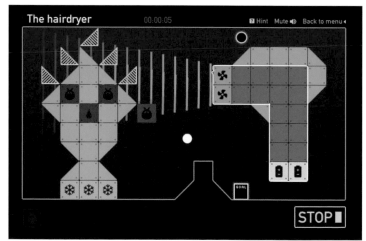

Figure 30
In the Launchball game, designed by Preloaded for the Science Museum in London, players have an inventory of tiles, each with a characteristic behaviour, such as magnetism, heat or insulation. When arranged correctly, the tiles create powered arrays that propel a ball towards a target. The game provides frequent feedback and hints to guide the player as each stage and level becomes progressively more challenging.

Gestalt theory

Gestalt is a field of psychology that is concerned with how humans make sense of the world around them. Gestalt psychologists are interested in how the mind organizes and groups together sensory information that appears to be similar or related. A large amount of work has been done to understand how we make sense of complex visual information. As far as gestalt psychologists are concerned, we do not perceive experiences as collections of separate fragments, but holistically, meaning as a whole.

Six principles of Gestalt

For many years now, psychologists have accepted that there are six cognitive principles at work when we encounter visual elements in a group. The six principles are potential tools that can influence our arrangement of visual information in a design. Alternatively, the principles may help diagnose how and why visual information is misinterpreted by users. These principles are: closure, continuity, similarity, common fate, figure and ground, and proximity.

An understanding of the gestalt principles of visual perception can help the designer create work that influences user behaviour, so that their navigation through a designed experience feels intuitive and rewarding.

Figure 31
Figure and Ground effects occur when we perceive objects to be 'stacked' one above the other. The image is perceived as a yellow circle on top of a white blob on top of blue circle (or a fried egg on a plate).

Figure 32
Proximity effects occur when objects that are close to each other are perceived to be related. The distribution of white space in this image suggests that this is three groups of car symbols, rather than nineteen separate symbols.

Figure 33
Common Fate effects occur when a number of objects appear to have movement or direction. The figures appear to share a common path, so they are perceived as either one figure at different stages of a fall, or several figures that are understood to imminently fall.

Figure 34
Similarity effects occur when objects look similar and are regarded as a group, even if they are not adjacent. The 'lemons' are scattered across the frame, but they are connected by their similarity.

Figure 35
Closure effects cause the mind to complete images that appear to be incomplete, finding closed shapes or patterns. Although these two cards and the background patterns are not delineated with borders, visual closure occurs so that we perceive the image as two stacked cards that are separated from the white stripes behind them, rather than as a single irregular white block attached to several 'combs' of attached white.

Figure 36
Continuity effects occur because of our inclination to see continuous lines rather than broken or adjoined lines. The blue 'Y' shape on the top is perceived as three lines joining in the middle. The red 'Y' shape below it, although similar, is perceived as two lines– a curved platform supported by a single stem.

Semiotics

Communication is accomplished via the exchange of small 'parcels' of meaning called 'signs'. Signs may take the form of spoken words and sounds; of graphical images and symbols; or they may take the form of gestures or body language.

Users are active seekers and decoders of signs. Everything and anything can be assumed to carry meaning. Even a blank screen is a sign (usually a sign that something has gone wrong). Semiotics is the branch of communication studies that is concerned with the relationship between signs and meaning, and it can provide us with insights into the opportunities for efficient communications, as well as warn us of potential miscommunication.

Certain types of signs are extremely arbitrary, relying upon a shared code in which a sign 'stands for' something entirely unconnected, such as a green light, which in many cultures means 'go ahead'.

These arbitrary signs are called 'symbols', and are based on a principle of mutual understanding that has evolved or been negotiated between everybody involved in the communication process.

Consequently, symbols are highly coded, meaning that if you don't know the rules of the sign-system, you can't understand the message. Symbols which are well known to designers and programmers may be part of a specific, acquired literacy that is unfamiliar to other people.

Icons and indexes are less arbitrary, more intuitive types of signs. It is possible to infer the meaning of an index or icon without prior knowledge of a shared code, because an icon has a visual similarity with the thing it represents, whereas an index has an alternative relationship with the thing it signifies (for example, a 'causal' relationship). Three vertical wavy lines could, in the context of a shower-tap, indicate 'hot water'. The lines may have an 'iconic' resemblance to rising water vapour, but the cause-effect relationship between the sign and what it means has a link that can be indexed. Recognition comes from our understanding that 'water vapour will rise because the water is hot'.

Constructing meaning from signs can be taxing on memory and attention, and may demotivate users. On the other hand, recognizing the 'language' of a new experience, particularly a novel technology, may be a part of the intrinsic pleasure of the experience.

Figure 37
These delightful icons from Robowolf illustrate how much pleasure can be derived from searching for the meaning in symbols.

Narrative

Experience is continuous. *An* experience is different. *An* experience has a beginning, a middle and an end. In order to define, recount and evaluate experiences, we need some way to delineate these from the constant flow of sensory experience.

Story and features

Story is one of the most fundamental ways in which we can mentally partition our experiences. The rules of systems that we use to organize events into meaningful and engaging stories is called 'narrative', and an understanding of narrative is ingrained in all users, even if they are not conscious of the structure. All previous experiences have shaped our expectations, and for thousands of years the principles of classical narrative have been observed in storytelling, literature and theatre. There are several features of a fully realized narrative:

A protagonist: a 'hero' or 'heroine' with a sense of purpose.

A goal: treasure to be found; justice to be served; order to be restored; love to be won.

A force of antagonism: a 'bad-guy' that gets in the way; a natural or supernatural force that provides conflict; a trait or flaw that threatens the hero's capabilities.

Causality: a pattern of cause-and effect in which the protagonist is an agent of change; things happen (desirable or not) because of the hero/heroine's efforts.

Resolution: a positive outcome; balance is restored to the universe of the protagonist.

These elements form the obvious structure of most novels and movies, as well as providing the underlying motivational logic of many games. But narrative is a structure that could be applied to many other interactive experiences.

We can regard users as the protagonists of their own experience. They have a goal to accomplish and may reasonably view the process of achieving this as a series of obstacles to be overcome. Users will regard themselves as the agent responsible for change, so we should do as much as possible to create the feeling that goals are achievable and actions are effective. When the goal has been fulfilled, the user should sense that balance has been restored; that their efforts have been fully resolved.

Commitment

Some experiences require a degree of orientation before the user feels fully committed: this corresponds to the 'equilibrium' that begins a story. Once the user is committed to the task at hand, the narrative journey is underway.

If we provide a user with a sense of where they are in their own narrative journey, they will be better orientated and motivated to proceed. By imposing or suggesting a narrative structure, we can make an experience more discrete and memorable.

Figure 38
The designers behind Upside believed that organizing a business trip shouldn't feel like an interrogation that spawns endless, identical-looking options. Brave UX considered how users may conceive the narrative of their trip as an analogy of the trip itself.

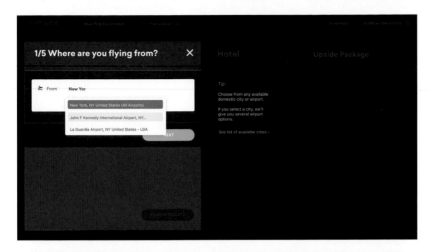

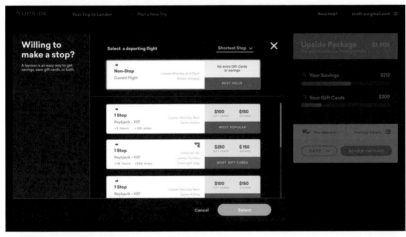

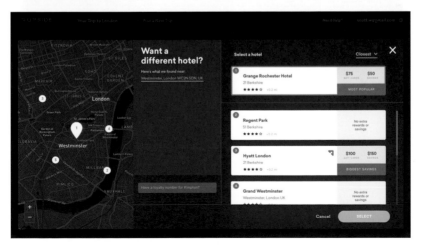

Constraints

A constraint is a consciously engineered part of an interactive experience that is designed to limit or influence user behaviour. Constraints may protect the user against harm, or error, or they may be part of the 'instruction' required to make sense of the experience.

Constraints are important tools for managing user expectations and minimizing user frustration. A client-side script that validates an email address; a 'wizard' that prescribes the sequence and scope of interactions; a 'warning' dialogue; these are all constraints designed to spare the user wasted time and effort.

A poorly conceived constraint may add to frustration and dissatisfaction. Constraints should match the users' mental concept of what is and is not permitted.

Where constraints are imposed, the reasons should be transparent and consistent. If a user feels that they are being denied legitimate choices, or admonished for legitimate actions, they may feel dissatisfied. A customer may be justifiably prevented from adding two-and-a-half tins of soup to their basket, but may feel frustrated if two-and-a-half kilos/pounds of tomatoes is not an acceptable choice.

The degree of constraint should also be proportional to the potential for error or harm. A 'no exit' sign is a constraint that discourages leaving by the wrong door. A turnstile does the same thing more forcibly.

Users accept and can even appreciate constraints. Often, constraints are there for reasons of safety and influence; sometimes they are imposed to create a challenge. The game of chess would be much simpler, but much less fun, if all the pieces moved in all directions.

It is because of the constraints that the user finds opportunities for learning and mastery which, if applied consistently and fairly, enhance an experience rather than diminish it.

Figure 39
At West Hill Primary School, playful signage invites the children to 'feed' items into their rightful storage spaces, and vibrant floor patterns encourage the children to sit in an orderly fashion. In products and interactive applications as well as environments, subtle constraints like these can influence user behaviour without being forceful or overbearing.

Activity #6

Recognizing intuition

It is generally considered high praise for an interactive design to be described as 'intuitive' by its users. The label 'intuitive' implies ease of use and logical operation that does not require the user to think. In fact, it is the user who is being intuitive, somehow knowing what to do in specific contexts when presented with a range of interaction choices. The designer has cleverly identified elements of the user's subconscious understanding of visual signs and processes.

It has been said that 'the only intuitive interface is the nipple' and that our lives from birth provide us with experiences that help us develop intuitive understanding that we can apply in different situations. If this is true, then designers can expect different intuitive responses from users with different life experiences.

Unfortunately, this means that a user interface that some find intuitive, others will find unintuitive. In this activity you will aim to recognize intuition similarity (or variation) between two or more users.

Steps

You will need plain paper, squared paper, scissors, a camera and at least two people to provide the user data (User A and User B). The activity can be extended for use with a wider range of users.

1 - canvas

Define an interface 'canvas' with a sheet of squared paper (10mm/0.4" squares are ideal). Users need to know that this represents the 'screen' of the interactive device; for example, a tablet or desktop computer.

2 - elements

Create 12 interface elements out of paper, each measuring 50 x 10mm/2" x 0.4". Write one of the titles from the list below on each element. Add a small arrow on elements that will typically take up a larger area than the paper element itself. The user can decide how much extra space to allow (see Figure 40).

Search

My account

Departments

Buy

Price

Sign-in

Choose quantity

Contact us

Sale feature product

Product photograph

Customer reviews

Product description

3 - user 'a' test

Making sure that User B is not able to observe or hear this step, ask User A to place each interface element on the squared paper in a position where they would intuitively expect to find it when visiting an online store. You will need to explain that the sheet of squared paper represents the 'screen' and the arrows on some elements mean that they need extra space (see Figure 41).

4 - record the result

When all the elements are in place take a photo of the 'screen', so that you have a record of the arrangement. Before removing the elements, draw a pencil outline around each one (see Figure 42).

5 - user 'b' test

Provide User B with the paper interface elements and ask them to place each interface element on the canvas inside one of the pencil outlines. They should position them in the space closest to where they would intuitively expect to find them when visiting an online store.

6 - compare

When User B has placed all the interface elements in position use the photo taken in Step 4 to identify differences between the layout created by each user.

7 - review

Discuss any differences in the choice of element layout with the two users. If the layout arrangements appear substantially different then continue testing with more users to build a better understanding of different intuitive responses. If the differences are slight, then the design already has some chance of success.

Outcomes

If this activity has been success   .ien you will have identified any differences in the intuitive response of the two users. Where conflicts do exist, these could be reduced by applying cues that are intuitive to both users, such as the use of scale and colour to create a visual hierarchy. Even a relatively minor change in visual design has the potential to change the user experience. Following the launch of a new interactive web design it is possible to carry out A B testing. This is a technique where a percentage of visitors are automatically redirected to slightly different versions of the same website and their actions are monitored.
⦿ uxto.me/a6

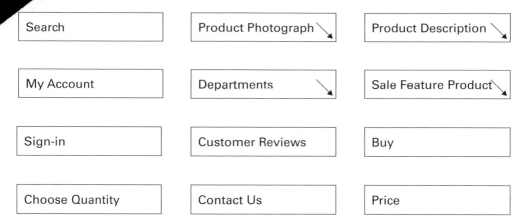

Figure 40
The 12 interface elements ready to be copied in Step 2 of the exercise.

Figure 41
A photo taken after User A has arranged the elements in Step 4.

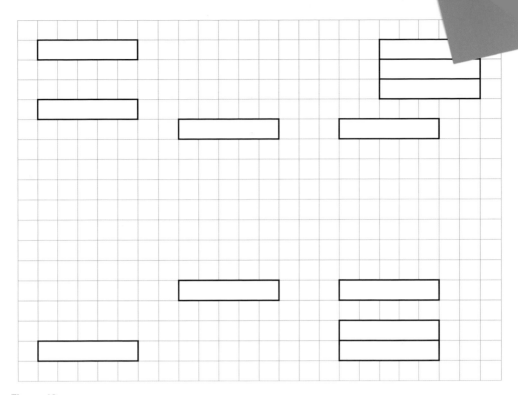

Figure 42
The canvas with outlines in which User B must place the elements in Step 5 of the exercise.

Design process

The products of a UX Design approach are analogous to a theatre show. When the experience begins, the audience seek entertainment. Oblivious to what has gone on prior to the performance, they expect a fulfilling experience. In the theatre, a bad show may be seen by hundreds. Online, a bad interactive design may be seen (and experienced) by millions.

Here, we look at the processes needed to manage and deliver effective designs. We look at the life cycle of a design and how user research and participation help shape the design specification. These activities can be time-consuming and costly, hence we introduce techniques to manage the process. In conclusion, we aim to show that good processes lead to better designs.

The life of a project

There are times in life when being creative comes first and thinking about the process of creativity is not important. We try to do things in some sort of logical sequence but sometimes we just muddle through. If the outcome isn't completely perfect then we can choose to do things differently next time, assuming we get a second chance and that everything else stays the same.

The purpose of a Process Model is to explain an approach that has proved to work well in the past. The model is usually graphical and uncomplicated, giving an overview rather than specific detail. It is not a plan but it helps in the development of a plan by signposting a sequence of actions.

A Google image search reveals that there are a lot of people out there with their own idea of a 'UX Design Process Model'. Typically, they have adapted an existing model in the light of their own experience. This is a good thing, firstly because it demonstrates that they have reflected on their own practice and secondly to show that models should not be regarded as sacrosanct.

Keeping in line with this thinking, Figure 43 shows the development of a model published by the UK Design Council. The original version is applicable to any design discipline. Our version applies some UX Design specific attributes, including the importance of user research and the need to iterate designs until they satisfy specific requirements. Let us know if you find it useful or have developed a version that works better for you.

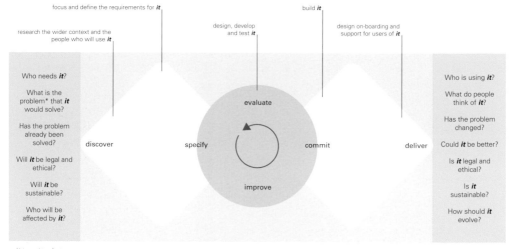

A design and development process model for something called *it*

Figure 43
Our own UX Process Model is a development of the UK Design Council's Double Diamond model.
◉ uxto.me/f43

User involvement

In Chapter 2, we briefly introduced the concept of user research and the identification of target users and their goals in using an interactive system. Good user research is needed to inform the design process, answering fundamental questions such as:

- Who are the users?
- What are the users' goals?
- In what context will the system be used?

The process

The design team will interpret the information gained through user research to develop a list of user requirements and generate initial design ideas. The process of interpreting user research is the first stage in an iterative design process. Iteration in this context means that the design is evaluated, the evaluation triggers improvements in the design, and then the design is evaluated again. This loop continues until the design is demonstrated to provide a good user experience that allows the target user group to achieve the required goals in specific contexts.

Evaluation

One way to evaluate a design is through user feedback and this is best done face to face, although there are many different ways that users can be involved. These range from participating in design meetings to being observed while interacting with design prototypes.

Iteration should be used to progressively eliminate uncertainty during the development of interactive systems. Iteration implies that descriptions, specifications and prototypes are revised and refined when new information is obtained in order to minimize the risk of the system under development failing to meet user requirements.
The International Standard ISO 9241-210:2010

In fact, there are two loops going on in the design process: the feedback loop and the design iteration loop. Improvements in design are dependent on the methods of evaluation applied and the insights that they produce. Involving users in constructive feedback is an effective way to provide the information needed to push the design process forward to successful completion.

The credibility of the design team is strengthened by carefully managed user involvement. For the feedback to be valid and useful it needs to be intelligently assessed in relation to the originally defined target users and their goals. The design team needs to prevent user involvement from shifting the design focus by, for example, adding features that are not required to achieve the user's goals.

Designing for human–computer interaction is exceptionally complicated and should probably be classed as exploration rather than design. As in any expedition to explore uncharted territory, it is a good idea to stop every so often, assess progress and confirm that you are heading in the right direction. If the design team were to do this too often then the project's progress would be slow and potentially disrupted by too many changes of direction. If done too infrequently, then the project risks being committed to a direction that cannot be changed due to the amount of work that would need to be undone and the time taken to backtrack.

The key to deciding when to iterate is the availability of new information coming from sources such as user research, technical reports or prototype testing. This implies that activities that generate this information are happening in parallel with the design activity – and so they should. The project leader needs to be the lookout of the team, metaphorically running to the top of each hill to survey the horizon and identifying when a change in direction should be considered.

Figure 44
What do people think and what do they consider to be important about your design problem? Cog organized this event so that researchers in their design team could run face-to-face activities with a group of potential users. The qualitative and quantitative data generated was analysed and helped to inform early design decisions.

Personas

Activity #2 is designed to reveal that designing for a diverse group of users in a range of situations is not an effective approach. In trying to create an interactive design that 'works for everyone, everywhere', a design team is most likely to create something that 'doesn't work very well for anyone, anywhere'. This is because the need to accommodate such broad requirements will result in either too much complexity or too little functionality in the design.

A better tactic is to target a small group of individual users located in appropriate contexts and to design just for them. In this way it is possible to focus on accommodating user characteristics that are similar. This approach makes the design task much less complex and the goal of creating a good user experience for the defined group much more achievable. Interestingly, the results of this approach often give an acceptable user experience to a much more diverse group than the target group identified by the design team.

What is a persona?

A persona is generally a fictional description of a model user based on high-quality user research of actual users in the target user group. It can include details about the user's education, lifestyle, interests, values, attitudes and patterns of behaviour. The persona will have a name too, allowing the design team to ask each other questions like, 'When does Sally have time to check her email?'

To allow for a range of users within the target group, it is generally considered necessary to create a number of personae (usually fewer than six). This allows the design team to consider differing characteristics such as aptitude, motivation and the context in which the interactive design will be used. Sometimes it may be useful to create personas of people who are not users but who are affected by the design. An example of this could be a parent who may be interested in the educational value of an interactive game for their child.

South London Gallery Personas

Cog. 15

Chris

If I had known the kids would enjoy it so much I would have visited sooner!

Age: 37

Location: Bexleyheath, Greater London

Occupation: Contractor / Site Manager

Marital status: Married

Children: 3 (young family)

Family-man

Driving • Aspirational

Background

Chris grew up in Brixton where he became a successful building site manager. 6 years ago he relocated to Bexleyheath to raise a young family.

Chris has high aspirations for his children and tries to keep them busy with fun and educational activities. He is well-paid and and has a large disposable income.

He has a very busy and tiring working week and the time he spends with children and family on weekends is incredibly important to him.

Motivations

Chris wants ideas for what to do on the day and would like to know what's available right now. He likes to organise a weekend activity when he visits family or with his children.

He wants things to be easy, simple, straight-forward and informative.

Website goals

Is the gallery open and what is on today.

Requirements or cost of children's activities.

Family friendly tone and advice.

Guidance on what experience will be like and what will happen.

Website frustrations

Upon arriving at the website it appears that it's not family friendly. Exhibition details and family considerations are not suited.

No direct information about on the day activities. Upcoming events require time to read into.

Symbols and indicators to distinguish areas would have been easier than text and sidebars.

Related content does not guide him to other areas of the site.

Does not know that the shop is family friendly.

Technology

Devices used to access the internet

Frequency of internet use
6 hours per day

Expertise

Internet

Mobile

Social media

Relationship

How well do they know South London Gallery?

not well ——————————— very well

What's their perception of South London Gallery?

negative ——————————— positive

Chris visits family in Brixton and regularly drives past the gallery.

He doesn't know that the gallery has great activities for children and family friendly events.

He wants to plan an educational and engaging day out for his children but would not normally think of the gallery as an option.

A positive experience is enough to convince him to return more regularly.

Figure 45

Chris is one of a number of personae created by Cog to help them better understand the people who will use a redeveloped South London Gallery website.

Scenarios

Personas can be given life by creating scenarios that feature them in the role of a user.

Scenarios are created by the design team to help them see the world from the user's perspective and can start simply and develop in detail as the project progresses.

They are useful because they allow the design team to place their ideas in context and to develop functionality that will meet the needs of the user. Creative writing and role-playing scenarios can also help communication and cooperation across the team.

Scenarios are written in the third person narrative style and usually start by placing the persona in a specific context with a problem to solve. The story develops by describing how the interactive product delivers what the user requires in order to solve the problem and achieve the goal.

In writing a scenario, it will start to become apparent what requirements are necessary for the interactive design to provide a good user experience.

When used alongside personae and interpreted in UX Design terms, simple scenarios like the one shown below can provide really useful pointers to a design team striving to provide a good user experience.

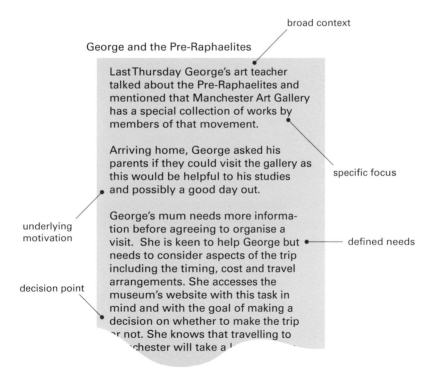

broad context

George and the Pre-Raphaelites

Last Thursday George's art teacher talked about the Pre-Raphaelites and mentioned that Manchester Art Gallery has a special collection of works by members of that movement.

Arriving home, George asked his parents if they could visit the gallery as this would be helpful to his studies and possibly a good day out.

specific focus

George's mum needs more information before agreeing to organise a visit. She is keen to help George but needs to consider aspects of the trip including the timing, cost and travel arrangements. She accesses the museum's website with this task in mind and with the goal of making a decision on whether to make the trip or not. She knows that travelling to ~chester will take a !

underlying motivation

decision point

defined needs

Figure 46
George's art gallery scenario can be dissected to reveal important aspects of the story as they relate to George's potential experience.

Figure 47
What do users hope to accomplish when they visit a website? Visitors to the web page of Manchester Art Gallery may wish to check the opening times, preview the collections, find out about special exhibitions, or arrange an educational visit for a large group. All of these potential scenarios, and others, are catered for in the uncluttered layout and unambiguous navigation

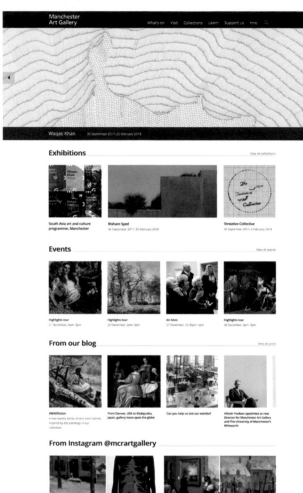

Activity #7

Scenario mapping

In Chapter 1 you were asked to consider a broad range of factors influencing the experience of people in a fictional story. In this activity you will write a scene within such a story – a scenario. In the same way as George's story on page 77, the scenario that you write will be used to test the effectiveness of a design intended to deliver a good user experience. This technique can also be applied in the early development of a new design. A well-considered scenario can help in the discovery process by imagining how the design fits in the world of a specific user.

Activity

Write a scenario about how characters (that you invent) are helped to do something in their world (that you also invent) by an app or website (that can be real or that you have invented). In UX Design terms this could be described as a persona in a context taking a user journey to achieve a goal.

You could start by choosing an online service and then imagining the person who would use it. Remember that in George's story it was his mum who actually did the online interaction and so you could think about similar situations. Alternatively, you could invent a character and devise a scenario that leads them towards a specific online interaction and work back from there.

George's story is about 100 words long, although it could usefully be up to 250 words. In just a few paragraphs it should be possible to discover what the interaction must do in order to provide a good user experience. Analysis of George's story can be used to test how well the Manchester Museum of Art website helps George's mum to make a decision and plan the trip.

Scenario map

After you have written the scenario you can extract information and ideas and map them across time.

The map of George's story separates the context, doing, thinking and feeling aspects of the scenario and places them within a nominal timeframe of a few days. Its purpose is to simplify and make visible the factors that could influence George's experience. When working in a team a map is much easier to discuss and develop than a piece of writing. In that case it may be better collaboratively using a whiteboard or sticky notes for the content.

If you are struggling with writing a scenario then there's nothing wrong with starting with a map. If you want to practice this technique before applying it to digital design, then why not create a scenario map of a scene in your favourite novel or TV drama? In order to be objective, write your scenario without referring to the design of the website or app. The headings shown should help in writing the scenario. The content alongside each heading relates specifically to George's scenario. You will need to think how this content can be adapted or changed to be relevant to your chosen app or website. When the written scenario is complete use it to map how closely the chosen app or website works to support the user experience. Is there anything missing or redundant? Does the flow mirror the narrative of the scenario? Does the design consider all of the experience touchpoints?

◉ uxto.me/a7

Scenario Map

Figure 48
A scenario map for George's story. Words with a negative prefix (-) are potential pain points. Ideas that could be developed further are identified with a positive prefix (+).

◉ uxto.me/f48

Design requirements

The payback for taking a UX Design approach is the amount of concrete information available to the team when actual design requirements need to be specified.

The work done to analyse data from user research activities will help to define the scope of the project and to provide focus for the project team. Techniques applied to understand users and their behaviour through personae and scenarios will also provide insights into the context of use. This is beneficial because it centres the design plans on the needs of users from an early stage in the project and places user experience at the forefront of everyone's thinking.

Where to start?

A good place to start the design process is by creating a list of initial design requirements. They are called 'initial' requirements because at the early stages of the process the team needs to take a flexible approach. A balance needs to be achieved between the requirement to provide a good user experience, the requirements of the client and the technical requirements of the systems on which the interaction will take place. In some situations, it is necessary to knowingly degrade the user experience to achieve a cost benefit.

From the user experience perspective, a requirement that the user interface employs a clean visual design with no distractions may be seen as essential. When considered from a commercial perspective the need to add links and advertising information may be critical

to success. There could be a technical solution that helps to reduce the negative impact on the user experience of a cluttered user interface. It is the job of the project team to recognize competing requirements and to use every tool at their disposal to achieve a balance.

Is there a better solution?

In any design process there can be a temptation to accept the first solution to a design problem. In our experience, students of design avoid looking for a better solution to a problem if an adequate solution seems to have been found. In an iterative design process, all ideas need to be challenged and evaluated after there has been an opportunity for them to be properly considered. If ideas are immediately challenged, then it will prove difficult to get the project rolling. By allowing time between the development of ideas and the start of a cycle of design evaluation, a project will have a chance to take shape. After formulating a strong set of design ideas, the project becomes a candidate for participation in design development and testing by users and evaluation by stakeholders.

Who specifies the requirements?

Team members will usually promote the needs of their particular area of expertise in the specification of requirements. It is essential to have a project leader who can provide a balanced perspective on user research, user interface design and technical developments to mediate and move the project forward.

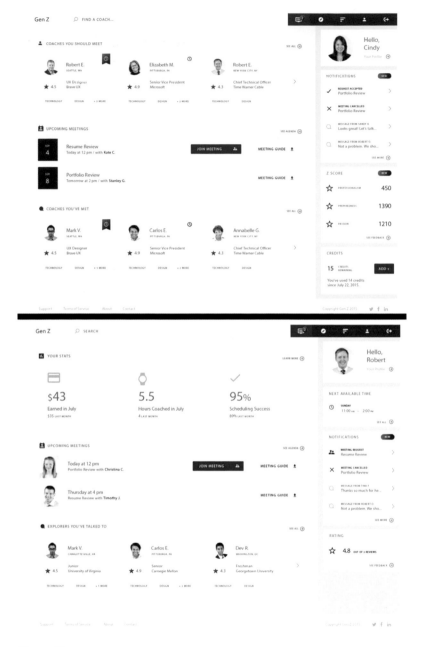

Figure 49
GenZ is a career-based networking platform. The interface has to work for both sets of users: students want to explore and pursue careers by connecting with experts (top); whereas professionals want to share their insights and identify new talent (bottom). BraveUX had to consider the full spectrum of requirements in their design for the universal navigation and information architecture.

Communication and planning

Effective project leaders are adept at encouraging excellent communication and morale in a project team.

They unite researchers, visual designers, interaction designers, technologists and programmers behind a common goal of creating interactive products that users really love. A good team will learn from each other and create design solutions that could not be conceived or developed without a multi-talented joint effort.

Planning

It is beneficial to identify specific stages in a project and plan for them well in advance. The careful scheduling of people and resources is needed to keep a project on track because team members may be working on multiple projects at different stages. For this reason, it is a good idea to keep the team size as small as is practical and locate team members so that they can meet easily and regularly. Project planning is an art requiring foresight and the ability to think along parallel timelines. Some tasks in the UX Design process can be undertaken at the same time or overlap other tasks. User research, stakeholder analysis and user modelling activities can overlap in most projects. It is a good idea to identify tasks that have the potential to hold up the project if they are not completed on time. For example, wireframes that visualize the underlying structure of an interface need to incorporate the functional elements of the design. This means that wireframe creation is an activity dependent on the functional specification being ready.

Aids to planning

Computer-based tools designed to make it easier to schedule tasks, match resources to tasks and identify task dependencies include Microsoft Project and Merlin from Project Wizards. Some really good web-based tools that offer team collaboration and file management features in addition to project scheduling are Basecamp (basecamp.com) and Trello (trello.com). Both companies offer free versions for smaller projects.

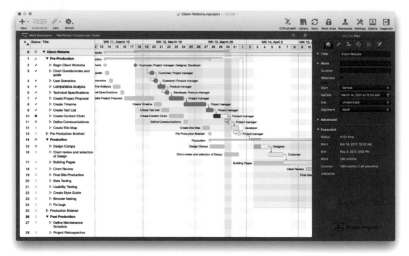

Figure 50
This Merlin screen visualizes project activity as a Gantt chart making it possible to see tasks, dependencies and responsibilities in parallel timelines that update automatically to reflect progress and changes to the workflow.

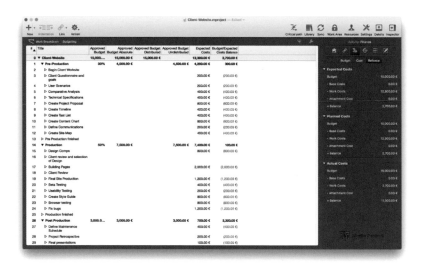

Figure 51
Project activities and costs are linked and brought together within this Merlin finance screen.

Design standards

When a new technology arrives, it is usually seen as a good thing, demonstrating human progress and perhaps an opportunity to improve people's lives. Sometimes the negative effects are not realised until harm has been done and lessons learned. Digital communication technologies continue to grow and take precedence. Alongside this growth standards have been set by community groups, government and industry to improve their use and reduce any harmful effects.

For a designer, working to standards is sometimes seen as a burden rather than a benefit, particularly when doing so requires design compromises. The potential consequences of a badly designed highway bridge can be easily understood. The impact of a badly designed interactive application is less obvious. Poorly designed and implemented applications have the potential to affect millions of users. The impact on people's lives can be just as serious as a vital bridge closed for repairs.

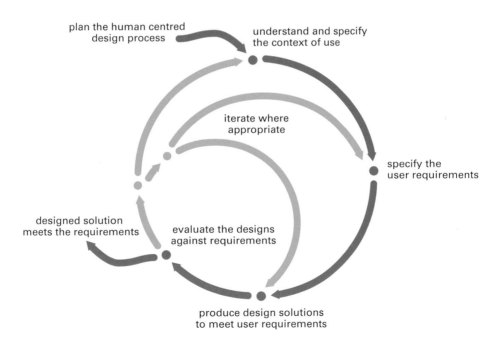

plan the human centred
design process

understand and specify
the context of use

iterate where
appropriate

specify the
user requirements

designed solution
meets the requirements

evaluate the designs
against requirements

produce design solutions
to meet user requirements

Figure 52
This diagram is adapted from one within the ISO 9241-210 document. It shows that user-centred design does not follow a strict linear process and illustrates that each human-centred design activity uses outputs from other activities. Design activities continue in an iterative cycle until the solution meets the requirements.

⊙ uxto.me/f52

In the early days of web design, accessibility requirements for websites were seldom considered by designers of visually rich sites. Where accessibility was considered, the technology in use often required users to revert to text-only pages. In 1999 the Web Content Accessibility Guidelines (WCAG) were published by the World Wide Web Consortium and this, together with updated HTML and pressure from disability groups, forced a change in thinking by designers and developers. When sites were redesigned to be accessible to those with a disability, it was often found that the changes improved the user experience for everyone – not just for those with sight loss, hearing loss, mobility or cognitive impairments.

From the designer's point of view, working to standards provides another way to show evidence of professional competence. Standards are regularly updated and so help to ensure that working practices are up-to-date and that designers apply the latest thinking in design and technology.

In UX Design, there are two standards bodies that have particular significance and, as in the case of web accessibility, have the influence to affect many aspects of interactive design.

1. The World Wide Web Consortium (W3C) (w3.org) is an international community where member organizations, a full-time staff and the public work together to develop web standards. Led by web inventor Tim Berners-Lee and CEO Jeffrey Jaffe, W3C's mission is to lead the Web to its full potential.

2. ISO (International Organization for Standardization) (iso.org) is the world's largest developer of voluntary international standards. International standards give state-of-the-art specifications for products, services and good practice, helping to make industry more efficient and effective. Developed through global consensus, they help to break down barriers to international trade.

At the time of writing, the international standard most relevant to UX Design is Part 210 of ISO 9241: Human-centred design for interactive systems. It is called Part 210 because it forms just one part of a group of standards within the Ergonomics of Human–System Interaction. Other areas include Part 11: Guidance on usability, and Part 920: Guidance on tactile and haptic interactions.

Part 210, which was reviewed in 2015, describes six principles of user-centred design and provides guidance on how to apply them:

The design is based upon an explicit understanding of users, tasks and environments.

Users are involved throughout design and development.

The design is driven and refined by user-centred evaluation.

The process is iterative.

The design addresses the whole user experience.

The design team includes multidisciplinary skills and perspectives.

Digital Service Standards

Worldwide, agencies of national governments, including the UK Government Digital Service publish Digital Service Standards (DSS). The UK standard currently includes 18 criteria 'to help government create and run good digital services'. All public facing transactional services for the UK Government must meet the standards, even those produced by external agencies and designers who are not public-sector employees.

The criteria are wide-ranging in their scope, requiring that the design process includes research, a multidisciplinary team, agile methods and an iterative process. There is an extensive service manual available on the government website. We include brief descriptions of the current criteria here and we encourage you to cross-reference topics that are explored within this book.

1. Understand user needs

Understand user needs. Research to develop a deep knowledge of who the service users are and what that means for the design of the service.

2. Do ongoing user research

Put a plan in place for ongoing user research and usability testing to continuously seek feedback from users to improve the service.

3. Have a multidisciplinary team

Put in place a sustainable multidisciplinary team that can design, build and operate the service, led by a suitably skilled and senior service owner with decision-making responsibility.

4. Use agile methods

Build your service using the agile, iterative and user-centred methods set out in the manual.

5. Iterate and improve frequently

Build a service that can be iterated and improved on a frequent basis and make sure that you have the capacity, resources and technical flexibility to do so.

6. Evaluate tools and systems

Evaluate what tools and systems will be used to build, host, operate and measure the service, and how to procure them.

7. Understand security and privacy issues

Evaluate what user data and information the digital service will be providing or storing and address the security level, legal responsibilities, privacy issues and risks associated with the service (consulting with experts where appropriate).

8. Make all new source code open

Make all new source code open and reusable, and publish it under appropriate licences (or provide a convincing explanation as to why this can't be done for specific subsets of the source code).

9. Use open standards and common platforms

Use open standards and common government platforms where available, including GOV.UK. Verify as an option for identity assurance.

10. Test the end-to-end service

Be able to test the end-to-end service in an environment identical to that of the live version, including on all common browsers and devices, and using dummy accounts and a representative sample of users.

11. Make a plan for being offline

Make a plan for the event of the digital service being taken temporarily offline.

12. Make sure users succeed the first time

Create a service which is simple to use and intuitive enough that users succeed the first time.

13. Make the user experience consistent with GOV.UK

Build a service consistent with the user experience of the rest of GOV.UK including using the design patterns and style guide.

14. Encourage everyone to use the digital service

Encourage all users to use the digital service (with assisted digital support if required) alongside an appropriate plan to phase out non-digital channels and services.

15. Collect performance data

Use tools for analysis that collect performance data. Use this data to analyse the success of the service and to translate this into features and tasks for the next phase of development.

16. Identify performance indicators

Identify performance indicators for the service, including the four mandatory key performance indicators (KPIs) defined in the manual. Establish a benchmark for each metric and make a plan to enable improvements.

17. Report performance data on the performance platform

Why you should report data and how you'll be assessed.

18. Test with the minister

Test the service from beginning to end with the minister responsible for it.

Activity #8

A design problem

In this activity, you will construct a solution to a simplified interactive design project in around 2–3 hours. The solution will take the form of an outline plan that can include a few rough sketches. The plan aims to describe a practical solution that satisfies the requirements of the design. It will explain the sequence of tasks that the user will need to complete in a path towards achieving their goals. The objective is to keep the burden of tasks to the minimum necessary to achieve the goals while also providing a good user experience.

A sample scenario identifying a user context is provided below, although this can be changed if required.

A university student in their final year needs to find information on opportunities for progression into employment or further study. User research has been conducted and user goals have been identified:

> to be aware of all relevant opportunities as they arise
>
> to have sufficient information to make informed choices
>
> to reduce the time spent filtering no relevant opportunities
>
> to save and recall specific information to allow later review
>
> to share specific information with others when required.

Steps

1 – understand the problem

Think of similar problems found in different contexts. Try to develop empathy with the user and think through their situation and why they would use your solution. Will your design communicate a shared understanding of the problem, instil confidence and function effectively?

2 – sketch ideas

Capture as many ideas as you can by using simple sketches and notes. If you are working in a group then set a target of 8–10 ideas from each person. At the end of half an hour ask each person to spend a minute to explain their best ideas. Choose one or two ideas to go forward to the next stage.

3 – identify the context

Think about how, why and where the user will access the solution. Consider the characteristics of the interactive system you plan to use. If you are not completely familiar with the system, then take some time to investigate the types of interaction available. A smartphone for example will generally offer a touch screen, haptic (tactile) feedback, geolocation, motion detection, voice control and audio/video functions for recording and playback.

4 – consider the content

An interactive application is made up of functional elements and informational elements. Functional elements need to be recognized by the user as controls or as part of the framework of an application. Informational elements, such as images and text, need to be recognized as passive content that may change but do not work as controls. There can be crossover between functional and passive elements. In some situations, an image can also be a control (e.g. to enlarge itself when clicked) and text can also be a control (e.g. acting as a navigation link).

Make a list of the elements you expect to see in the application and identify them either as functional or informational. Keep an eye on where these elements are used and review their status as functional or informational. Think how the user will understand what type of element they are by the context in which they are found and their appearance.

5 – architecture and structure

Define the entry point and the interaction options that you are providing for the user. Write down what the user can see and what the user can do. It will help to draw simple boxes representing the interface elements.

Identify how the user goals are brought closer for the user by following each of the interaction options you have defined. From this point forward, you are constructing the solution and creating the experience. If any of the interactions do not advance the user forward to one or more of their goals, then consider changing or removing it.

Draw a map that plots every possible user interaction option and make a connection to the result of choosing that option. Show how the user takes a journey along the path towards achieving their goals. Continue until you have created a solution that appears to offer a route to the achievement all of the user goals.

Tip:

Have you considered that new users of the application may need a different entry point than existing users? What sort of information may the user want to see before continuing with their interaction?

6 – validate

Invent a few individual user scenarios like the ones below to test your solution and see how it performs.

'Dave is sitting in a cafe with a friend from his course. At the end of their current courses they both want to progress to a relevant postgraduate course in the USA. They each study different subjects but want to stay within a four-hour drive of each other so that they can meet up at weekends.'

'Gemma is a student graphic designer and wants to find a graduate-level job in London. She is aware that any opportunities are quickly snapped-up and wants to be alerted to new ones as they arise so that she has the best chance of making a successful application.'

Tip:

Is the user able to form a logical mental model of the interaction path that you are designing? How hard is it for the user to undo a simple mistake such as choosing the wrong option or mistyping something?

7 – iterate

Review your solution and improve it until you are confident that it works reasonably well for the individual user scenarios that you have invented.

8 – test

You now need to make your ideas accessible for others to test. You will need to convert your notes and sketches into something that a user can recognize and interact with. Activity 12 is designed to help you do this.

Result

If this is your first attempt at designing an interactive application, then this activity is likely to have been revealing and probably quite difficult. We expect that you were slightly frustrated by the minimal information provided in the problem definition, the lack of detail about the interaction framework, and the difficulty of achieving user goals. If you think that you need to go back, improve the user research and define the problem more closely before starting to develop solutions, then that is probably true. If you think that you have a better understanding of the problem by attempting to solve it, then that seems likely too.

Activity 12 expands on this activity by taking a design solution through to the prototyping stage. A real project staffed with a UX Design team of perhaps 4–9 people would spend much more than 2–3 hours on a problem like this. To aid the process they may run a Design Sprint; a highly structured and time-limited group activity that continues over a number of consecutive days.

⊚ uxto.me/a8

Figure 53
Slides from the Google Project Design Sprint deck help
teams to organize and run an effective design sprint.

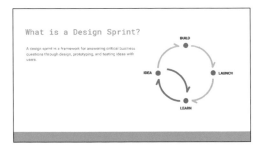

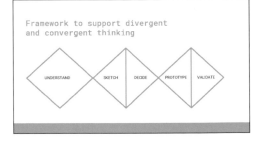

5

Design constraints

The reality of human experience is that there are constraints; physical boundaries and social attitudes that limit what we can do. Understanding constraints and working within them requires skill and knowledge developed through experience. In many ways a design problem can become easier because constraints limit the range of possibilities for solutions, providing more focus for the design team.

In this chapter we'll help you to identify constraints in simple design problems and think about how to handle them.

Aesthetics

Aesthetics is a branch of philosophy concerned with the nature of beauty. For thousands of years, intellectuals and artists have debated where beauty resides, and the extent to which the beauty can be attributed to universal and indisputable characteristics.

Because the term aesthetics can encompass so much, it is, ironically, often used in a way which has little useful meaning. It is a term that is too often used to describe or justify intuitive or arbitrary design decisions. The phrase aesthetically pleasing may sound like an educated judgment of a design outcome but used in this way it does not explain how conscious or informed design choices have been made. It offers no rationale behind the design process which produced the work in question.

An alternative use of the term aesthetics is to categorize design values into recognizable design movements, styles or epochs. For example, a font may be described as having a futuristic aesthetic; an illustration may depict an Art Deco aesthetic; a style of layout may observe a punk aesthetic. When aesthetics is used in this way, it is acknowledging the historical and cultural context in which designs are devised, created and experienced. When we encounter a website, and app, a poster, a movie title sequence – in fact, any sensory experience – we bring to that experience a wealth of prior experience and memory which influences our notions of aesthetic satisfaction.

These era-specific attributes are not intrinsic: a font, illustration or layout cannot be imbued with an in-built sense of time or place. However, they may embody certain visual signifiers which the users may consciously or subconsciously associate with other experiences.

Many aesthetes argue that artistic originality is a fallacy and that it is impossible to create art which does not in some way emulate, duplicate or respond to pre-existing artworks. Any response to our designs will be experienced in relation to contemporary or historic design trends; this is inevitable.

When we think about aesthetics, we must consider what has preceded our work. Whilst we may have an infinite number of digital typefaces to deploy, it is easy to forget that in the not-too-distant past, typographical decisions had practical and technical implications which constrained and defined the aesthetic for a generation. Similarly, the technology that afforded colour printing was, in the past, constrained by affordability, as well as the availability of limited pigments. It is necessary for the UX Designer to become cultured; to recognize key movements in design history, and the technological advances that have delineated these movements.

If aesthetics can vary to mean everything, nothing or something, how can it be of any use to us as designers? Like so many aspects of UX Design, aesthetics represents another opportunity to look outside of ourselves; to consider the broader context in which experiences take place, and to recognize that the designer is not the adjudicator of what does or does not look nice.

Figure 54
Wordpress Themes
Two contrasting Wordpress Themes from Premiumcoding showing how variations in colour, type and imagery can create distinctly different aesthetics using the same underlying platform.

Although the debate about aesthetics continues to occupy the academic and artistic communities, several aesthetic maxims have been established. These maxims form convenient rules-of-thumb which we can use as design strategies or as diagnostic tools in our daily practice. These universal principles of design are not obligatory, but have been recognized, time-and-again, to result in harmonious visual and spatial arrangements.

Proportion

If you visit an art gallery and study the collections of paintings which may span thousands of years of artistic endeavour, you will observe one common feature. Typically, the artworks fill a rectangular area, either in landscape or portrait orientation: one side is longer than the other. With the notable and challenging exception of some smart-watches, it is unusual to see a non-rectangular display on a computer, tablet, or mobile device.

Some experts concerned with the detail of aesthetic principles have gone further to specify exactly which height-to-width ratio is the most ubiquitous and most appealing. This proportion is called the golden ratio and has been accepted as a reliable unit of special relationships in design. The ratio is approximately 1:1.61. It appears frequently in nature, and even in the dimensions of the human body: the division of the human hand into the regions of the fingers and the palm observes this divine ratio; the wrist divides the forearm and the hand at a similar ratio; throughout the body, this proportion recurs.

When the ratio is applied to progressively increasing intervals, the result is a sequence of numbers which map onto the spirals of shells, seeds, and even hurricanes. Aesthetes argue that evidence of the golden ratio and its variants in nature explain why we favour this proportion in art and design. It has been revealed as a structural feature of revered works of art from the Great Masters. It can be applied to external boundaries of a frame or view-port, but also to the internal subdivisions of a design, such as margins, anchor-points or columns of text.

Colour harmony

We know that music can be composed of tones of different harmonies. Analogous to tones in music are the colour components of light, which, like music, can be combine in harmonious ways.

A simple way to visualize the possible relationships between colour groupings is to use an artist's colour-wheel which depicts the colour spectrum as a clock-face of hues. Colours paired from opposite sides of the wheel are called complimentary colours. A colour scheme assembled from adjacent hues is known as an analogous colour scheme. A triadic colour scheme combines three hues which split the wheel into 120 degree portions. There are a range of tools available to the designer that help in the selection of harmonious colour schemes for visual displays and printed works.

Figure 55 Vitruvian Man (circa 1490)
A drawing by Leonardo da Vinci based on the writings of Roman architect Marcus Vitruvius Pollio. The work illustrates the proportions of the human body, with the navel located at the centre of a circle. Awareness of ratios and naturally occurring symmetry are important factors to consider in your approach to design.

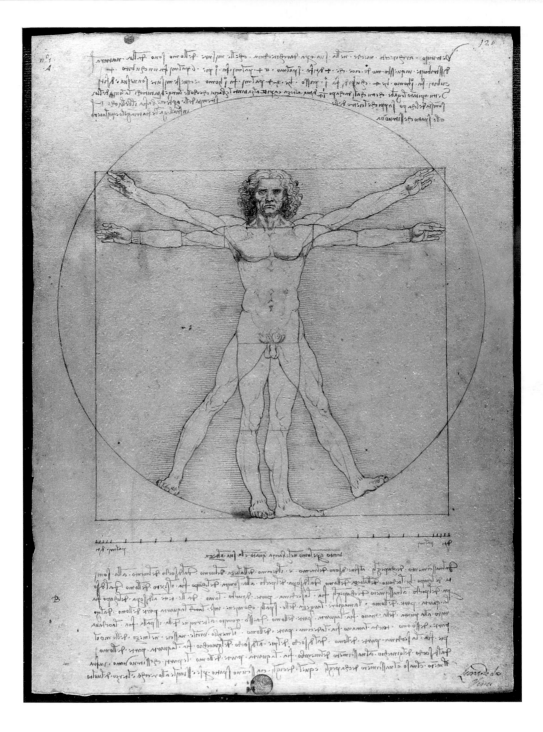

Figure 56
The design agency Rotate° imagined a luxury yachting experience starting with the first click of the website they designed for Helm. Visitors answer a series of simple questions to create their uniquely tailored holiday.

Meeting the requirements

When embarking on a design project, the objective is to produce the required outcomes for clients, users and stakeholders. This rather obvious statement hides an uncomfortable fact that design teams can sometimes lose sight of the required outcomes. Instead, they may focus on meeting requirements that have crept into the design process since the required outcomes were identified through user research.

The team needs to be clear about what it is they are designing, what the user requirements are, and what functionality needs to be created in order to fulfil the user requirements. Beyond this, they also need to consider client, stakeholder and technical requirements.

Requirements statements

Once the desired outcomes of an interactive design are understood, it is useful to define the requirements in a 'requirements statement'. This document will typically be managed by the UX Design project leader and become the focus for those with responsibility for creating the design and achieving the functionality. They also serve to inform the client about what the project aims to deliver within the agreed budget.

A 'requirements statement' will usually have a hierarchical structure, with essential requirements at the top of the hierarchy and supporting requirements lower down. Because the design process is iterative, it is very likely that the statements will need to be revised during the development stage of the project. The possibility of this happening can be reduced by:

- Maintaining a clear focus on the user experience rather than on developing features
- Applying the best design approaches to achieve the required functionality
- Linking and simplifying different requirements, e.g., creating a responsive design rather than multiple designs.

Semantic design

An experience can be thought of as a journey during which we will interact with different types of digital information. For example, a user may retrieve a catalogue entry for a product, upload and collate some photos, watch a video, write a review, or edit a wiki article. Each subsequent encounter adds to the residue of digital data. Every artefact in this mass of data is a unique resource with the potential to shape the user experience, but this will happen only when the information is arranged in a meaningful way.

The purpose of semantic design is to devise a data-model, or Information Architecture (IA), for organizing information in a way that makes sense to people. It also defines the language (or syntax) for the systems that will store, link, exchange and interpret the data in order to personalize our experiences.

When applied to designed experiences, semantics describe the way in which information is organized and interconnected in a meaningful way.

More and more experiences are going to be powered by this data. Users will need to find, retrieve, aggregate, create, edit and contextualize information with ease, and the experience will need to be researched and designed with this in mind.

Metadata means 'data about data', and it is embedded into digital documents: file names, properties and ownership are all types of metadata.

In social media settings, we can often tag our information with pertinent metadata in order to contextualize it for a wider audience or to label it for future reference. Metadata is one of the means by which we can organize information in a way that makes sense to us.

Figure 57
Cog Design worked
closely with their
client to develop an
architecture for the
Akram Khan Company
website that meets
the needs of a range
of users.

Figure 58
Cog Design's solution is a site structure which does not rely on complex navigation or extensive
sub-sections. The site was then developed around this hierarchy, creating a site which exploits to full
effect the images and videos of the renowned dance company.

Figure 58 (*continued*)

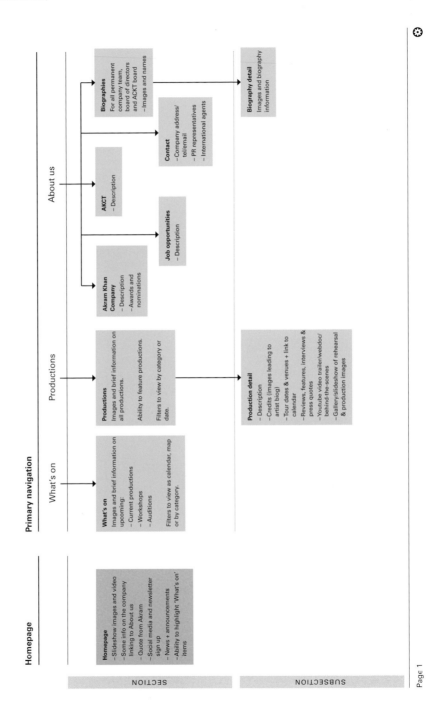

Akram Khan Company siteplan

Design patterns

In some situations, users will enjoy an innovative and unusual interface. They will delight in the process of exploring and discovering what they need to do to interact and navigate through the content. Along the way they will learn the language and controls of the interface and subconsciously commit this knowledge to memory. When they return they will know what to do without the need to explore.

Creating and customizing

The human capacity to recall an interface design can offer designers a shortcut to creating new interactive designs that are already familiar to users. Design patterns are reusable templates that include elements of structure and control that are widely understood. They can be customised to meet specific requirements while keeping the use pattern intact. This has advantages in common user interface situations such as controlling navigation, making selections and submitting requests. Design pattern libraries sometimes attempt to identify the context and the ubiquity of specific designs. Often, they exist simply as collections of interface graphics, sometimes with variations for different action states; highlighted, selected, visited and so on. They can also exist as software libraries that include code that drives the functional as well as the visual pattern. Interactive designs created as applications will often incorporate interface elements provided by the host platform's development environment. This is why user controls to select a date or choose a value from a list appear identical in many applications on the Apple iPhone but are handled differently on Google Android and other smartphone systems. When developing for these platforms a designer will need to justify the use of alternate design patterns to those provided by the system. Reasonable justification could include the need to offer additional features or innovative interaction designs.

Problems with design patterns

The use of appropriate design patterns can benefit the user experience but there are some pitfalls to avoid.

If the design pattern uses interface elements that are unfamiliar to the user then they will need to learn and remember what they are for and how to use them. A Sony PlayStation controller includes symbols that are abstract and require the user to develop an association between the symbol and the function it controls. In some cases, the function changes with the context of the interaction. Designers need to provide support for first-time users of interactive applications so that abstract or hidden controls can be discovered and learned. Other problems can be caused for the user if the use pattern is modified. When the user recognizes a design pattern and expects it to behave in a certain way – then it should.

Figure 59
Patternry Open is a library of user interface patterns offering
examples, guidance on usage and, in some cases, example code.

Activity #9

Recognizing UI patterns

As human users of websites and apps we focus on our purpose for interacting rather than the process of interacting. It is only when things refuse to work as we expect that we start to look more closely at the virtual buttons, tabs and other controls that drive the interaction. This activity is designed to reveal how well you know common user interface (UI) design patterns and their behaviours. The purpose of the activity is to help you think about the most appropriate pattern to use in any given situation. This requires both a good knowledge of existing patterns and an understanding of the subtleties of their operation.

Keep away from the computer, tablet or phone and, using paper and pencil, sketch one or more of the design patterns in the list below. Annotate the sketch to explain how things work and how the user is assisted to achieve their purpose without thinking too hard about the interactions. If necessary, draw a sequence of sketches to show how the interaction progresses.

1 An email sign-up form that appears in a modal window.

2 Navigation tabs that appear above the content on a website.

3 A product slideshow that appears in a frame beside a product description.

4 The interface controls that appear around the live image in a smartphone camera application.

Hints for each example

At what point does the user know that the information entered is acceptable? If the user does not want to register, how easy is for them to dismiss the modal?

How can the tabs accommodate long descriptions? How does the user know which tab indicates the current view?

How can the slideshow be clearly understood to be related to the product description? How can the user choose to see close-up images of parts of the product that they want to inspect closely?

How are the controls arranged so that they do not obscure the view of the scene being photographed? Which of the controls are most important?

Review your work by comparing to it to patterns in use within a mainstream website or application. Did you recognize the subtleties? Is your design better?

⊚ uxto.me/a9

Figure 60
This SVG Avatar by Darin Senneff shows how animation driven by the user's actions can turn a simple sign-up form into a mini comedy. As the form is completed the avatar changes expression and seem to be watching the user's movements. A visual punchline comes when the avatar shields her eyes so as not to see the password.

Email

email@domain.com

Password

Log in

Email

email@domain.com
Gavin

Password

Log in

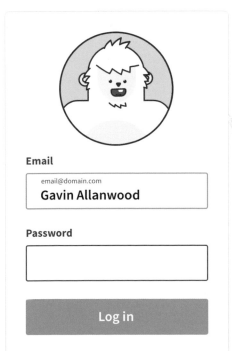

Email

email@domain.com
Gavin Allanwood

Password

Log in

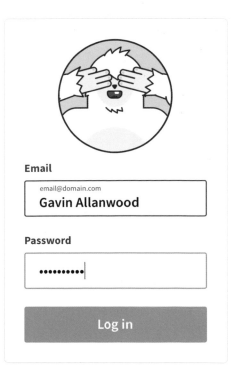

Email

email@domain.com
Gavin Allanwood

Password

••••••••••

Log in

Layout

Layout is the strategic arrangement of the elements in a visual design. It is the harmonious placement of type, image, line, shape, tone, colour, imagery and space. Layout can be applied to books and magazines, web pages and electronic documents, as well as interfaces, environments and controls.

The purpose of layout is to: create attractive visual relationships between elements; to organize (group/separate) visual information to make it easier to understand; to create emphasis, so the most important information is not overlooked; and to create direction, so that information is encountered in the correct order.

User research is an important tool in evaluating a layout. For example, observing or interviewing the user may reveal cultural factors that influence how they interpret or prioritize visual information. On a more quantitative level, eye or gaze-tracking technologies allow us to measure how users navigate their way through visual information, so that we assess with some confidence whether or not they are providing the best visual experience.

Brand awareness may also be a factor in designing a layout. Decisions about colour, type and space may be influenced by corporate guidelines that stipulate how logos may be combined with other visual elements.

Layout should be unified and consistent. Separate pages or screens have a shared framework so that users will recognize they belong together despite their distinctly different content. Grids are a common way of creating this unity of visual design. A grid is a lattice of horizontal and vertical guides that are distributed across the page or screen. During the visual design stage, the grid provides a series of intersecting 'anchor-points' onto which the visual elements can be placed.

Grids are usually constructed around established divisions and proportions. The grid guidelines are only visible to the designer, who will remove or hide them once the layout is satisfactory. A flexible grid is one which allows for variety in the arrangement of elements in different ways whilst preserving a recognizably consistent underlying structure and hierarchy.

In the early days of the World Wide Web, designers struggled with the screen as a replacement for print media because they were frustrated by the fluidity of the medium. Compared to layout for electronic media, layout for the printed page is comparatively straightforward. Although it requires a great deal of visual awareness, it is a singular task, as the dimensions, orientation and proportions of the page are fixed; the content is designed to occupy this static canvas visible at once as any overflowing content is reserved for the next spread rather than occupying an 'overflow' space beyond the visible canvas.

By contrast, designing for the screen is often not a matter of making all the visual elements 'fit' into a limited canvas. Devices with varying capabilities for interaction and wildly differing screen sizes provide a real challenge for designers.

Layout for electronic devices is a more multi-faceted challenge than print-based design, as the same material may have to be repurposed for displays of different dimensions or orientations or respond to changes in the user's context. The layout may have to flip, rotate, scale, minimize, resize or change order completely, depending on the capabilities of the display equipment.

Consequently, the information design can be considered independently of the constraints of the device on which it is viewed. Electronic media can be thought of as an infinite canvas of information, with the user display acting as a tiny 'window' through which fragments of this content may be viewed. Users may have to be reminded of off-screen notifications that can be pulled into view as required. Some visual information may be context specific, so it may be fully or partially hidden at times. Alternatively, the information may be presented in series, fragmented into screen-size units.

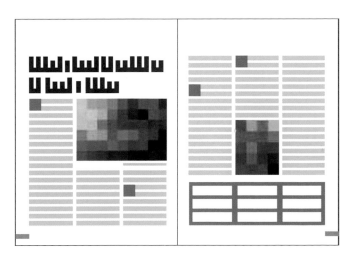

Figure 61
Digital layout is not a simple matter of organizing elements on a screen of fixed dimensions, as if designing for a printed magazine spread.

Figure 62
The device may act as a window upon a much larger canvas.

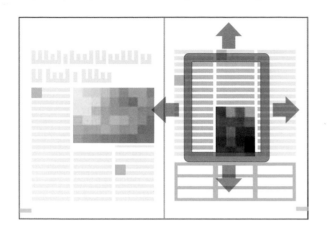

Figure 63
The components of a digital
design may need to scale.

Responsive design

Another approach to layout is to automatically rearrange the material to better suit the medium. Fortunately for designers, it is possible for a system to query a device's capabilities before presenting any media on it. This means that, with some intelligent coding, a visual design can be dynamically adjusted to provide appropriate content for a particular device or platform. It also means that designers can create designs that are relevant to the device and the context in which it is being used.

Developer tools for Apple apps include a feature call Auto Layout which automatically adjusts the user interface to respond to changes in size and orientation of the specific device being used. Similarly, materials assembled using HTML exploit a media query function to determine the size of the display area and apply a style sheet to organize the content accordingly. It is important to remember that there is a dynamic relationship between the information, the medium, the user and the context; these interact to influence the best presentation format.

The following types of textual or visual information have traditionally been presented in a fixed format on paper of appropriate dimensions:

- A novel
- An illustrated magazine article
- A city map
- A ticket or security pass
- A recipe

For each object in the previous list, consider what kind of adaptation is most appropriate for display on a wide range of devices, from a watch to a connected TV. Is it appropriate for the content to be rearranged into screen-sized portions or does it make more sense for the screen to act as a window onto a full-sized image that can be re-positioned? Should the context and the user interface of the device affect the fundamental design of the work? How has the layout problem been addressed by designers who work with these type of objects?

Although there are many principles of layout which can be migrated from the realm of print, users are now active stakeholders in the presentation of media. With the power to intelligently recognize the user's preferences, and even the capability to assess environmental factors, layout for UX Design results in arrangements that are more sensitive, more bespoke and more rewarding.

OUR FEATURED COLLECTION

Backpack for any opportunity
£90.00

ADD TO CART

Mountain Shoes
~~£235.00~~ £189.00

ADD TO CART

Special Coffee Mugs
~~£45.00~~ £42.00

ADD TO CART

ABOUT US

WE ARE BRITONIC

CREATIVE STORE

Hello, we are **Britonic**. We are enthusiast bloggers with our own set of hand made products.

FASHION. PHOTOSHOOTINGS

BRAND NEW SELECTION OF FASHION

No products in the cart.

NEWSLETTER

Sign up to receive updates and join our 3 subscribers that see what's new with Britonic!

Enter Email Address...

SUBSCRIBE!

F ashion is a popular style or practice, especially in clothing, footwear, access, makeup, body piercing, or furniture. **Fashion** is a distinctive and often habitual trend in the style in which a person dresses. It is the prevailing styles in behaviour and the newest creations of textile designers. Because the more technical term costume is regularly linked to the term "fashion", the use of the former has been relegated to special senses like fancy dress or masquerade wear, while "fashion" generally means clothing, including the study of it. Although aspects of **fashion** can be feminine or masculine, some trends are androgynous.

BACKPACK FOR ANY OPPORTUNITY
£90.00

OUR FEATURED COLLECTION

Backpack for any opportunity
£90.00

ADD TO CART

Mountain Shoes
~~£235.00~~ £189.00

ADD TO CART

Special Coffee Mugs
~~£45.00~~ £42.00

ADD TO CART

FASHION. PHOTOSHOOTINGS

BRAND NEW SELECTION OF FASHION

Figure 64
This Wordpress theme from premium coding illustrating how the site would look in a wide window (above left) compared to a narrower device (above right).

Image

Images, especcially photographic images, can add tremendous value to an experience. Images can act as visual aids to assist memory and understanding. Images can shape user expectations by giving them visual models of what lies ahead. Images can illustrate the preferred mode of interaction, so that the experience is more intuitive and less frustrating.

Images can exist as digital files to be located and retrieved for display on devices of various dimensions, or they may be printed on packaging or surfaces of fixed dimensions. Different types of image display require different methods to be applied when they are devised and created. Displaying images, particularly moving images, can require considerable resources to be available for transmission and display. For this reason, image files are usually compressed by removing information that is not normally noticed by the viewer in a way that does not degrade the experience of viewing the image. Planning an enjoyable, image-rich experience requires an understanding of these technical requirements and many others.

In addition, there are a number of factors to consider at various stages of designing an interactive experience that uses static or moving images:

Which devices or surfaces will the image be displayed upon? What are their capabilities for handling and displaying images?

How can the image respond to different devices and platforms?

How is the quality of the image related to the quality of the user experience?

Is image metadata required to utilise the image?

What is the communication function of the image?

Will there be any environmental conditions that affect the fidelity or meaning of the image?

What emotional impact, positive or negative, will the image have on the user? Images can be a very seductive element in any experience; interactive applications, print and environmental.

This is not to say that an experience always lives up to the promise of the image used to represent it. In recent years, publishers, advertisers and consumers have been more alert to the ways in which images can deceive. For example, airbrushing and manipulation of images in software such as Photoshop can create unrealistic ideals of beauty or health. In addition, unimaginative or ill-informed choices of images can reinforce harmful attitudes, such as the prejudice caused by misrepresenting different cultural and ethnic groups.

Unrealistic imagery can create unrealistic expectations, which will inevitably lead to disappointment. This can have a negative impact on individual self-esteem, and even on society in general. Images should be used in a way that promotes a realistic portrayal of the world and our place in it.

Copyright

Copyright is a set of principles, backed up by various international laws, whereby the creator of an artistic work can authorize or restrict the re-use of their work. Copyright applies to images, written works such as poetry and lyrics, typefaces, and even some types of performance. As designers, we have a legal obligation to respect creator rights, and we should only make use of images where permission has been explicitly granted for the image to be used.

Permission is usually obtained in exchange for a fee, and sometimes the rights to re-use an image may be negotiated directly with the creator.

Image rights are often handled by agencies who offer searchable databases of easily licensed photographs and illustrations. In a project which involves the use of many images, a picture researcher may be employed to contact copyright owners and negotiate the scope and terms of image use.

Securing expensive copyright licences may be beyond the scope of a small-budget project. Fortunately there are some lower cost alternatives such as Creative Commons, a licensing system whereby the permission to re-use or adapt a creative work is clearly expressed. Creators can assign a Creative Commons licence to their work, permitting reproduction, modification and commercial use. Search results within Google Images and Flickr can be filtered so that only unrestricted or Creative Commons images are displayed. It is important to check the wording of the licence for conditions of use. It is typically a requirement to include image credit text that correctly attributes the image to the source. Unsplash is an online collection of high-quality images provided by photographers without any restriction. Popular images hosted on Unsplash are typically downloaded millions of times and are therefore unsuitable for projects that require original and fresh images that have not been seen in other contexts.

Figure 65
The Wild Weather app combines accurate forecasts with charming hand drawn
illustrations. Although many alternative apps also provide reliable meteorological
information, Wild Weather demonstrates how elegant and evocative imagery can add
value to the user experience.

Figure 66
Online stock photographs are generally protected by copyright, and fees are usually required to reproduce them in any form. The photos made available on the Pexels website are licensed under the Creative Commons Zero (CC0) license. This means the pictures are completely free to be used for any legal purpose.

Type

Typography is the art of selecting, combining and arranging different typefaces in order to create structure and meaning. When typography is used well, the appearance and placement of words can communicate just as much as the words themselves.

Typography can be used to create visual repetition, in order to create a relationship between sections of type that may be spatially disconnected.

As well as possessing a distinctive personality, type can be adjusted to create contrasts in scale, colour and direction. White space around characters, words, and lines of text can also be adjusted to affect how the text will be perceived. In this way typography can create a visual hierarchy and organization. Sensitive choices about type can lead the eye around a page or screen, thus giving emphasis to particular pieces of text and encouraging users to interact with specific elements.

Type can be a very powerful visual instrument for creating emotional responses. Users can often identify very strongly with different categories of type. Some digital typefaces can have the appearance of erratic hand-drawn lettering, creating a sense of freedom and individuality that may resonate very strongly with the reader. Conversely, elegant and geometric typefaces may provide a reassuring sense of orderliness, reliability and of efficiency. Users of business or legal services will have their expectations reassured by an appropriately business-like typeface.

Many familiar typefaces come pre-installed on computers or bundled with software. Alternative typefaces can be downloaded, licenced, installed and used on specific devices for the production of designs for print. Typefaces used for web designs are now typically integrated from cloud services such as Google Fonts, which at the time of writing offers 858 font families that can be freely and easily coded into online designs.

In order for non-standard typefaces to render correctly on a device they must be coded within the application, available online or locally installed. Designs will not appear as the designer intended if the system does not have access to the relevant typefaces. This is one more reason why designs should always be tested outside the development environment and in the context of use.

Figure 67
Design agency Analogue designed a bespoke logo for the menus of The Hummingbird Kitchen and Bar. The design was also forged into a striking exterior display proving that type can be a tangible and unifying element of an experience.

Accessibility

In UX Design we consider that there is no archetypal user. We will already be alert to the context in which experiences occur, and to the needs and motives of the users. However, we must be particularly sensitive to the universal accessibility of our designs. We have professional, ethical and legal obligations to ensure that the experiences we create do not exclude users with disabilities. Users must be able to perceive and interact with experiences, regardless of any sensory or mobility impairments they have.

The World Wide Web Consortium have developed a set of standards for creating accessible content called the Web Content Accessibility Guidelines (WCAG). Although the guidance is primarily for intended for use by developers of web content and tools, they provide a useful reference for accessibility of many experiences, including mobile-friendly accessibility. Even for offline experiences, such as events, or board games, the guidelines can be used as an empathic provocation to help consider any obstacles the designer may overlook.

One important principle of the WCAG advice is that no harm must result from design choices. Although flashing elements may serve a useful purpose to alert users to errors or hazards, these have been known to induce seizures in people with certain conditions, so a maximum frequency of three flashes per second is recommended. Another key principle is that materials must be navigable: not only to users with the mobility to manoeuvre a mouse or to press a touch-screen, but to users who may navigate through items using their keyboard only, or alternative assistive technology. Therefore, content should be organized into a logically hierarchical structure so that users (and the assistive technologies they rely upon) can make sense of presented material. Contextual information about interactivity should be included: for some users, it can require significant effort to engage in a single click, so ambiguity should be considered and minimised. For the same reason, experiences should be predictable, lest any futile effort be wasted on an inconsistent action or outcome.

All elements should be perceptible and distinguishable. Whereas text elements can usually be interpreted by screen-readers employed by users with visual impairments, the presence or function of images are often unclear. It is good practise to provide a textual alternative description of images, so that it is apparent whether they are informative or merely decorative. Equally, audio alerts and instructions are of little use to users with hearing impairments, so these should be conveyed in an alternative or additional medium.

For the UX Designer, considering disability should not be a perfunctory observance of legal duty to a minority population. Disability is a significant dimension of the lives of many of us, or the lives of others who matter to us. The spectrum of disability may interact significantly with other demographic characteristics of users; for example, certain impairments may be more likely in the elderly.

These accessibility guidelines are not exhaustive. And, even with all principles considered, it may be very difficult to mitigate against all obstacles for all users. However, recognizing the importance of accessible design is an important step towards becoming designers with greater creativity, empathy and respect for the user.

Figure 68
Signly is an app that generates a smart layer of signed or spoken filmed digital information on the screen of a visitor's own mobile device. It animates, translates and invigorates the experience of d/Deaf sign language users and people with sight loss by making essential information accessible.

Activity #10

Onboarding

The term 'Onboarding' has been adopted from the field of human resource management where it is used to describe those situations when a new employee needs to acquire specific knowledge and become socialised with their workmates. In UX Onboarding enables people to start using an application quickly without reading or learning too much. Successful approaches to onboarding show the user how to achieve their goals in the context and logical flow of the application. In this activity you are going to apply your new-found knowledge and appreciation of UX Design to create an onboarding process for a first-time user of a new interactive application.

In the last activity you were asked to sketch a familiar user interface pattern from memory. When comparing your sketch with the real thing you may have overlooked some subtleties in the design. This is probably because you have subconsciously learned the interaction process after the first few times of use. You know how it works without thinking. Normally there would be no reason to re-learn a familiar interaction but as a UX Designer it is essential to start with a clean slate. Correctly applying widely recognized design patterns is a good way to reduce the risk of user interface issues. Even when design patterns are applied it is sensible to test their effectiveness with potential users who sit outside of the design team. Use this activity and the Duolingo example to see how interface patterns can be applied to make users think about the content and not the controls.

Duolingo

In Chapter 2 we introduced Duolingo as an example of motivational design, delivering a game-like experience when learning a new language. Here we show how Duolingo onboard new learners almost instantly. Their approach removes the friction of a sign-up form and has a new user learning a language in five taps or less. The focus is on giving the user what they want. How the system works is progressively explained and sign-up is not required to get started.

Steps

Design the onboarding process for a gift-wrapping service accessed via a smartphone application. Items purchased from an online retailer can be routed for delivery via the wrapping service. What do you think the user wants? How can you motivate them to engage in the service?

1 – problem solving

Analyse the Duolingo example and user narrative. Follow the approach outlined in Activity 8 to get started with your design.

2 – prototype

Develop prototypes from paper through to a simple interactive mock-up using software (e.g. Keynote or PowerPoint). Test and refine.

3 – review

Is your solution frictionless, quick, effective, painless? How can it be improved?

◉ uxto.me/a10

Figure 69
A journey through the main steps of the Duolingo
onboarding process shown in sequence with an
imagined user's 'inner voice' narrative.

1

Free forever? How can they do that? It will
probably take me forever to learn French so
that's a good feature. Let's see what Get Started
does. . .

2

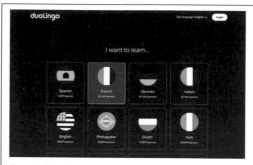

French is what I want to learn. I'll click
through . . .

3

Commitment! Can I learn a language in just 10
minutes a day? Unlikely!

4

Well let's just see what's on offer first! I'm not
sure I trust you with my life story just yet. Not
now Duolingo . . .

5

Basic. Really basic!

6

Photos! So a woman is 'la femme'. I thought it was 'madam'!

7

That was easy! I seem to have started learning already. It looks like I have 5 or 6 more questions to answer . . .

8

This is really good. I can cheat!

9

I'm ready to sign up but let's keep this separate from Facebook for the time being.

Mindset and toolset

Because a UX team is multidisciplinary, including people with diverse skills, there are a correspondingly diverse range of tools and ways of thinking applied to create great user experiences. The team needs to contain people with competence in the most effective tools and techniques to drive all aspects of the development.

There exists a dynamic landscape of resources to assist UX Design teams and in the following pages we highlight some considered core and others that are really very niche. It takes time to assemble a 'UX Design kit' for your own area of specialism but it's a good feeling when the tools you have chosen save you time and help you to produce better results.

Platforms and technologies

A digital media platform is a system that users recognize as a distinct way to interact with digital media applications. The platform can often be independent of the hardware device. Facebook have worked hard to develop their original website into a social media platform that can be accessed on the Web through smartphone apps and through other devices such as smart TVs.

Users recognize Facebook as a place to communicate and share different types of media. Designers adapt the Facebook interface to provide a similar experience to users across a range of different devices. Users modify their expectations of what they can do with Facebook when using devices with different capabilities, screen sizes and input methods.

The Web is an open platform that can support a wide range of technologies and devices. Complex websites accessed through a browser can be developed to the level of a platform. Huge sites such as Facebook, eBay and Amazon all fall into this category. When responding to a client brief to provide a new website, it is a good idea to consider the limitations of an isolated website approach. A project may be more successful from a UX Design perspective if delivered as a web application within an existing platform, such as Facebook, or as a mobile application that can work on a range of devices and the Web.

Applications built on existing platforms provide benefits for the user, including authentication (no need to log in), a familiar interface, opportunities for shared experiences, and access to services provided by the platform, such as user registration and geolocation data. Benefits for the client include access to large numbers of potential users, built-in payment systems and opportunities to market their business through social media.

Figure 70
Augmented Reality (AR) apps have the power to add extra value to all types of experiences. Arart is a stunning example of how AR can enhance activities in the physical world. The software uses a device's camera to recognizes images and brings them to life with inventive animations. In this example the app is being used to animate the Girl with a Pearl Earring, an oil painting by Dutch Golden Age painter Johannes Vermeer.

Communications and organizations

Good communication is often cited as the hardest thing to achieve in teamworking and it can take effort by the project leader to encourage everyone to discuss and embrace the challenges of experience design.

Members of the team need fluid communication channels, where they can share expertise, put forward ideas, work collaboratively and post status updates. Face-to-face meetings are important but need to be structured and managed so that they are also positive and productive.

It may be necessary to support other members of the team in developing their communication and interpersonal skills, particularly if they are unfamiliar with a UX Design approach. The project leader needs to be good at listening and able to recognize the importance of what it is being said, to moderate discussions and to help maintain a balance between competing interests.

Many excellent software tools are now accessed through the Cloud via software as a service (SaaS) subscriptions. It's worth remembering that SaaS generally requires a continuous fast Internet connection and that if problems hit the company providing the service then they will probably affect you too. For this reason and to keep potentially sensitive data off the public Internet many companies still choose to use locally installed software.

Project management tools can help a group to manage multiple projects. Redmine (redmine.org) is an open source tool offering facilities to chart a project's progress, post documents and manage files. It can also track time spent on activities as well as technical issues in software development. With over 2.5 million accounts, one of the longest established and popular SaaS offerings is Basecamp (basecamp.com).

Scrum is a tightly structured 'agile' software development framework that includes daily team-based decision making and prioritization of activities. There are a wide range of SaaS tools that specifically support a Scrum framework, including Scrumy (scrumy.com/about) and Jira (https://www.atlassian.com/software/jira) which can also be installed locally.

Project schedules are traditionally managed using Gantt charts that show project activities as a number of parallel timelines identifying resource use and duration. Each timeline can include events such as start dates, end dates and milestones in the development of a project. Tom's Planner (tomsplanner.com) is a popular SaaS Gantt chart tool which is simple and easy to use. Microsoft Project which is part of Microsoft Office is a full-featured Gantt charting tool aimed at business users.

Figure 71
Basecamp is a productivity tool that makes it much easier to see and understand what work needs to be done, when it needs to be done and who needs to do it. A single communication thread maintains a record of the process, ensuring that collaborators and managers have the information that they need without recourse to email or paper notes.

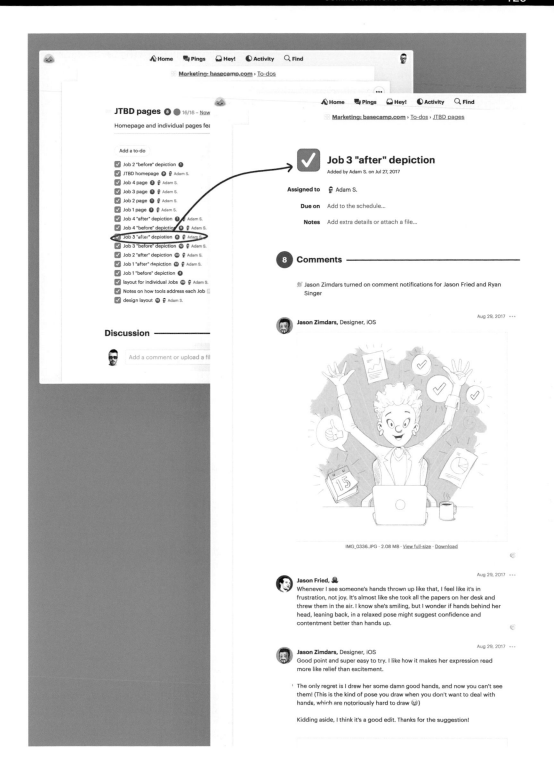

Empathy

Putting yourself in someone else's shoes is an expression used to help us comprehend the idea of empathy – the ability to understand what another person is feeling from their perspective. A UX Designer without empathy fails to recognize fundamental needs and risks alienating their human users.

For some people being empathic is a part of their character; for others it is invisible and recognizing the experience of others will require self-development. Being empathic is part of a UX Design mindset. It is a quality that can be improved through the use of tools and techniques. The creation of scenarios and personas (see pages 76–77) can help a design team to develop common empathy because they are techniques that encourage a wider understanding of the target user group. Bringing users together with designers and developers early on in the project will also help to foster an empathic response to their situation.

Studying users in the field is a good way for designers to get out of the studio and start to empathise with users in contexts that are relevant to the project in hand (see pages 22–23).

Empathy tools can be used to simulate barriers that may exist for particular groups of users. When designing for users with special conditions or disabilities, designers can wear devices that simulate the users' experience. Putting on a pair of weighted shoes can help designers understand the barriers facing people with mobility problems. When designing for people with impaired vision, wearing a pair of cloudy spectacles can help designers discover how well their designs work for that particular group of users. The effect of these activities is to enlighten and stimulate creative responses that would otherwise remain untapped.

Figure 72
These glasses have been developed as an empathy tool for designers to experience a general loss of the ability to see fine detail. The effects are representative of problems such as an inability to achieve the correct focus, reduced sensitivity of retinal cells, and internal parts of the eye becoming cloudy. These effects typically occur with age-related eye conditions, as well as not wearing the most appropriate corrective glasses. One pair of glasses simulates a mild loss of vision. The thin and lightweight design makes it possible to simulate more severe levels of impairment by wearing multiple glasses on top of each other.

Figure 73
These gloves have been designed to help designers empathise with those with dexterity impairment. The harder a product is to use while wearing the gloves, the more demand it places on dexterity and the more inaccessible it is. Conversely, if a product remains comfortable to use while wearing these gloves, then it is likely to be more accessible for a broad range of users.

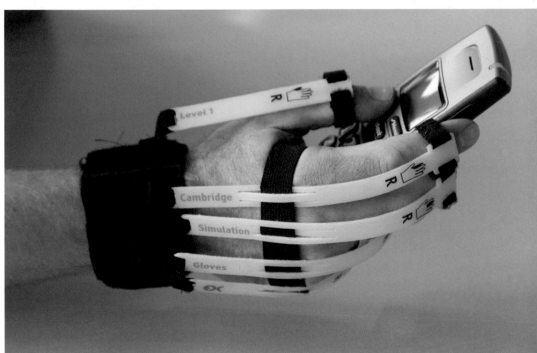

Ideation

To be a creative designer, we must be able to 'on demand' think up new ideas of some benefit or value to others. Recognizing how tough this can be, advertising executive Alec F. Osborn argued that "it is easier to tone down a wild idea than to think up a new one". His philosophy informed an ideation technique he called 'brainstorming'. Its core principle is to split the ideation process into two distinct phases: the first is the development phase; the goal is to create as many ideas as possible, no matter how outlandish. The second phase is the evaluation phase; the resulting ideas are assessed more soberly or reinterpreted in order to make them more feasible and practicable.

A large whiteboard is a good tool to record ideas generated by groups. Flip-charts are good for sequencing ideas; individual sheets can be torn out and easily reorganized, passed around a group and edited. Smartphones are great for recording and distributing hand-written or hand-drawn materials in these group ideation sessions.

In practice, a brainstorming session can be difficult to run, as it can be hard to suspend our critical judgement, particularly of other people's ideas. A designated moderator can encourage the proliferation of new ideas, and discourage the premature critique of suggestions.

Your group may be more productive if they are trained in strategies for creating the fanciful ideas in the first place. Edward De Bono, who coined the term "lateral thinking", suggests that tactical provocations can produce new ideas. 'Reversal' is one such provocation, whereby we consider a familiar axiom or truism and 'flip it on its head'. For example, if we consider the convention "the customer reviews the product", a reversal becomes "the product reviews the customer". At first glance, this sentence is gibberish, but if we treat it as a creative provocation, we can begin to interpret it as a potentially ambiguous description of a clear idea.

What could this mean? How could a product review a customer? Well, perhaps the product would have to monitor how frequently it is used, by whom, and for what purpose. This might yield data that could be used to gauge the suitability of the product for the customer. Perhaps it could adapt to become more beneficial, or could itself recommend alternatives, or even substitute itself. By applying such a line of reasoning to a deliberatively provocative statement, we can arrive at ideas with potential for improving experiences or creating new ones.

In his books on the subject of creative thinking, De Bono explains additional provocations, such as exaggerating one aspect of the problem, or using random words or other stimuli to elicit new perspectives or associations.

One way to guarantee you can produce a good idea when you need one is to create an 'idea bank'. This may be a collection of found artefacts or self-generated notes, photos and sketches. There are a number of digital tools to assist with collecting these inspirational materials. Evernote or Microsoft OneNote are examples of programs for capturing and organizing ideas. However, a notebook or flip-chart can serve this purpose equally well. Sketching is by far the most fluid and dynamic way to capture and communicate thoughts. Even simple sketches can illustrate ideas, put sequences in order, map relationships, indicate scale and suggest alternative options. Many people are more than a little self-conscious about sketching. Perhaps they do not want to reveal what they are thinking! Regardless of whether you use paper and ink or a smartphone app, the additional advantage of maintaining an idea bank is that it will help you hone your powers of observation. You will become more aware of the types of experience we engage in each day, and of the pleasures and frustrations that result. As a consequence, you will become a more sensitive, more alert and more resourceful UX Designer.

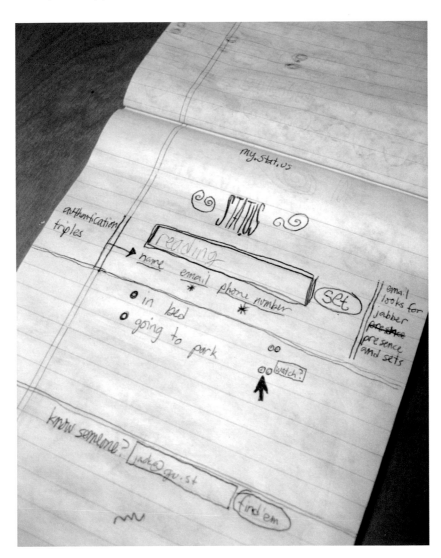

Figure 74
Jack Dorsey's 2006 sketch idea for twttr, now known as Twitter.

Problem solving

Staring into space waiting for inspiration to strike is not a very purposeful or cost-effective way to seek out creative solutions to problems. A more systematic approach is more likely to generate multiple solutions to the problem at hand. A good starting point is to take care to define the problem without imposing a preconceived solution upon it.

Imagine that we face this problem: flight departures are delayed, at some expense to the airline, because passengers frequently arrive late to the correct gate. We could articulate this problem thus: "we need to clarify the gate information on the departure boards". However, by phrasing the problem like this, we have presupposed that the solution will involve visual communication or graphic design. As a result, a variety of other approaches will be overlooked, such as penalties for late arrival, or rewards for promptness. If the problem is framed with a greater degree of abstraction, additional creative avenues may open up.

We can achieve this abstraction by asking ourselves 'why?' a number of times.

We need to clarify the gate information on the departure boards. Why?

Because passengers arrive late to the correct gate. Why?

Because they are far from the gate when the gate is revealed. Why?

Because they are waiting at the distant end of the terminal. Why?

Because it is a more comfortable waiting area. Etc.

With every progressive deconstruction of the initial problem, we reveal new dimensions, each one of which presents a new potential starting point for our problem-solving campaign.

A critical lens

Once we are content with the various ways in which the problem is defined, a critical lens is required to examine the problem from different perspectives. The tactical provocations (reversal, exaggeration, random stimuli) referred to in the previous section on 'Ideation' can be used for this stage.

This book can serve as a critical lens with which to interrogate a problem. For example, you could randomly choose a page and discover the topic of semiotics. Using this as a prompt, you could focus on the ways the user makes meaning of the experience under consideration. How might the experience be improved by reviewing or redesigning these meaning-making cues? Is there any ambiguity or complexity that could be eliminated? Or is it possible that greater ambiguity would enhance the experience by injecting more of a challenge?

The first right solution

Once we have arrived at a qualifying solution, it is easy to consider the problem-solving phase complete. Why waste any more energy searching for a solution when we already have one? Good designers are tenacious and resilient, pushing their problem-solving efforts in order to find better solutions. They aim to produce designs that are distinct from their competitors, and provide a really good experience for the people who use them.

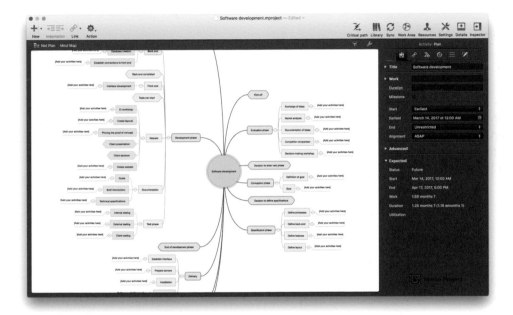

Figure 75
Project Wizard's Merlin software offers a way to create a conceptual version of a project as a mind-map, and can apply this structure to automatically create a project plan.

Activity #11

Visualizing data

This activity is designed to help demonstrate the value of sketching in a UX Design context. A sketch is a quickly produced drawing that make ideas or abstract data visible. Because ideas can be fleeting or transient the important thing is to capture them before they disappear or are forgotten. For most people the best way to sketch is to make marks on paper with a pen or pencil. For this activity use whatever works most quickly for you – traditional or digital. It is not important that sketches are done neatly. If they have merit, they can be developed into slick maps, graphics and design templates later on. There are two parts to this activity. Allow at least 30 minutes for each step.

Steps

1 - data gathering

Imagine that five friends are starting a journey to meet you at your current location. You know where they all are at the moment:

> Dave is at your favourite local coffee shop.
>
> Aroon is at the nearest large grocery store.
>
> Camila is at the nearest passenger sea port.
>
> Colin is at the nearest international airport.
>
> Zola is at the nearest emergency hospital.

Hopefully you have an idea of the approximate distance and direction of all of these places relative to your location. If not,

then ask someone with local knowledge for help. As a last resort, guess!

On the largest piece of paper you can find, sketch a map with your current location at the centre. Try to sketch in such a way as to show a range of multidimensional information, for example:

The location and distance of each friend as they start their journey towards your location and the form of transportation they may take.

Award yourself a point for each piece of information that can be derived from the sketch, for example: Where friends may cross paths and the combined travelling distance of all your friends. If you are doing this activity with others, then perhaps compete to see who can achieve the most points.

Figure 76
A quick sketch visualizing the five journeys suggested by Activity 11, done in about ten minutes with much use of a pencil eraser. The digital version took a little longer and was produced because it can be easily edited for the different language editions of this book. If you think that the sketch is too simple to be useful then consider how much writing would be needed to communicate the same information. How easy would it be to remember?

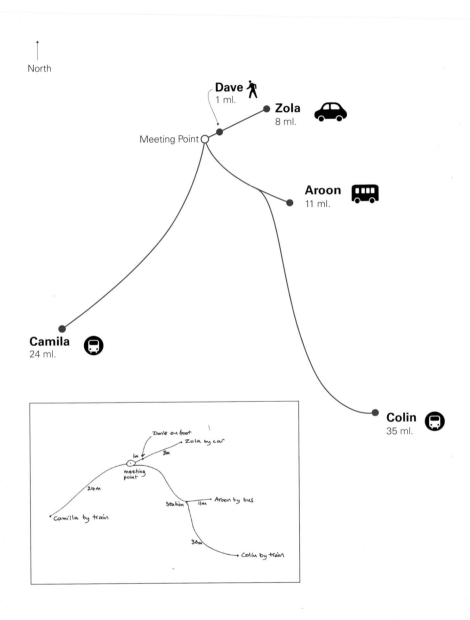

North

Dave 🚶
1 ml.

Zola 🚗
8 ml.

Meeting Point ○

Aroon 🚌
11 ml.

Camila 🚏
24 ml.

Colin 🚆
35 ml.

Dave on foot
Zola by car
1m
8m
meeting point
24m
Camilla by train
Station
1m
Aroon by bus
36m
Colin by train

2 - sketching

Let's stretch our imagination further to the day when an artificial intelligence-powered application can accurately calculate the best time for each of your friends to depart, summon an autonomous vehicle and deliver them to your location. In the previous step you have already begun to think about the human and logistical factors of the situation. The act of creating the sketch has hopefully worked as a catalyst and visualized the scenario. Now, while the factors are fresh in your mind think about the design of the app. How will it work to reduce the burden of planning individual journeys? How could it improve the experience of its users? Perhaps it could proactively design routes where friends travel together or accommodate last minute changes of venue for the meeting?

Make some quick sketches of your ideas. These could include simple interface designs that show the flow or a map of the interaction architecture or just a sequence of interface states. However you choose to do it, remember that as well as sketching ideas on paper to externalise your own thoughts, you are also developing a process to communicate your ideas to others.

◉ uxto.me/a11

Maps and flows

Tools that help visualize the flow of an interactive system allow a team to develop and rcfine the underlying architecture. Diagrams and charts offer a good way to analyse interaction scenarios and remove potential problems at an early stage. Some tools make it possible to automatically map existing websites by following all possible navigation options and displaying them in a linked hierarchical chart. Flowcharts and diagrams can be hand-drawn or created using software tools such as Creatley (creately.com) or Microsoft Visio.

Storyboards are traditionally used in linear film-making where they are used to visualize a script in a sequence of hand-drawn scenes. They are also used in interactive design as a quick way to visualize an interface and describe a typical sequence of events in its use. Printable templates for storyboarding are available online or can be easily created. Presentation software such as PowerPoint or Keynote can be used for storyboarding and also provide options for easily sequencing storyboard frames in a non-linear way.

Figure 77
Detailed sketch notes are a fun way to record and communicate thoughts, inventions, events, discussions, processes and a host of other things that are too difficult to remember and put into words. They also survive software updates and can be easily communicated with a smartphone camera.

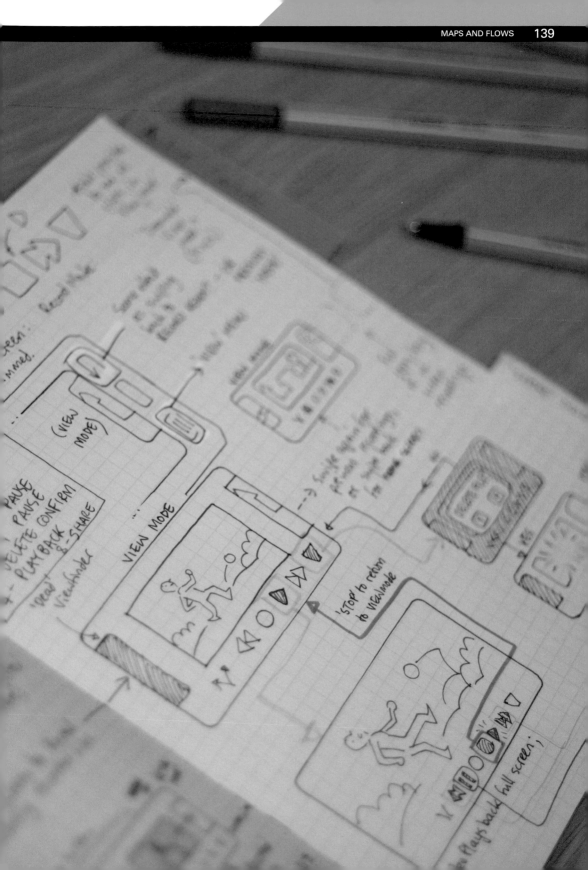

Figure 78
Sticky notes are a UX Design favourite for exploring navigational flows and structures. Not all notes have the adhesive qualities required, so choose your brand carefully and remember to photograph the work as it progresses and definitely before leaving the building!

Working with users

Conducting user research is potentially the most time consuming and costly aspect of a UX Design approach. Any tool or technique that can help you get a better understanding of your users is better than none, particularly if the results are reasonably accurate and the cost is low. Time spent with users can be supervised, for example in face-to-face meetings and workshops, or unsupervised, such as when users respond to an online survey or provide feedback on a prototype that is accessed online. Supervised time is generally referred to as moderated and unsupervised activities are termed un-moderated.

Before recruiting a pool of users to engage in initial research that is specific to your project, consider what can be achieved through desk research and data gathering. Organizations such as the UK Design Council undertake ethnographic research into particular topics and the results of these are made available to designers.

◉ uxto.me/6dc.

Card sorting is a user activity that can deliver insights into what users expect from an interactive design. Elements of the design are described on individual cards and the user is asked to arrange them into a logical structure. Card sorting can be moderated or un-moderated with sessions delivered face-to-face or online. Optimal Workshop offers an online tool for running remote card sorting sessions (optimalworkshop.com).

Contextual inquiry is a tool of user research that aims to provide a realistic view of users and their environment. It involves spending time with users and observing their activities in the context of the proposed interactive design. This could be at home or at work or in a specific situation, such as using a public transport ticketing system. A well-designed contextual inquiry will reveal aspects of the user experience that will be missed by other forms of research, but it is expensive to undertake.

A content experiment is a way to test different versions of a live website. The design team can receive minute-by-minute reports of their success in delivering goals for the user and for the site owners. The method is a development of A-B testing where two versions of a web page are compared by alternating their availability to users.

Content experiments allow discreet changes to a web page's content to be made and tested. Content experiments make it possible to measure the reaction of users to different visual and interaction elements and refine designs in an objective and quantifiable way.

Google leads the way in website analytics and content experiments.

◉ uxto.me/6go

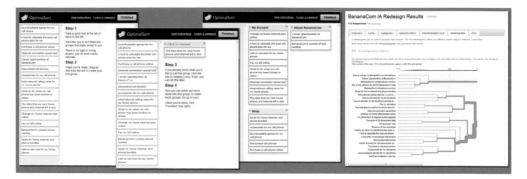

Figure 79
OptimalSort is a web-based card sorting tool from Optimal Workshop. In this example participants are asked to group the information and functions offered by a telecom company's website. Users can drag cards (the statements on the left) into a blank space on the right to create and name a new collection. Users drag more cards into a collection, create more collections and move cards between collections to visualize their idea of the site's information architecture.

Prototypes

A UX Design prototype is a model used to test a concept or process. The main benefit of a prototype is that it helps the design team learn how well their design performs. If there are problems or scope for improvement it helps to identify what further work is needed to make it better. It is quite normal for elements of a design to fail completely in a prototype leading to rethinking and radical improvements in the design. Prototyping is an iterative process, meaning that the results of testing one prototype are used to improve the next. The process iterates until the design works as required. Sometimes it is useful to create prototypes for different parts of a design. In a large project it is likely that prototypes will be produced for the visual design, user interface, media content, interaction architecture and for the code that makes everything work.

Prototyping is an activity that needs to be fast and flexible. Prototypes should be made cheaply and quickly so that changes in the design do not cause significant extra time and effort. The value of prototyping lies in the readiness of the design team to re-think ideas at an early stage if good results are not achieved. A flexible approach encourages innovation because the risk of failure is not serious. The work involved in testing multiple prototypes is preferable to proceeding to production with a bad design.

A prototype can be any form of model of the proposed design. It could, for example, exist as a flow chart, a stack of cards, sketches or slides. It is even possible for someone in a team to role-play the action of software – a human powered prototype.

Mock-ups

A UX Design mock-up is a simulation
of a proposed design. Its main purpose
is to demonstrate a design to project
stakeholders and potential backers. A
sophisticated mock-up will effectively
simulate the function, look and feel of the
final product or service.

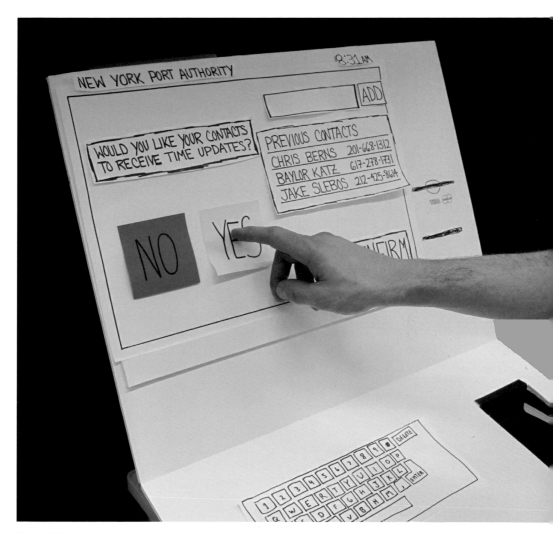

Figure 80
Paper prototypes are the ultimate low-fidelity approach to making an interface real and allow simple
testing of your designs.

Activity #12

Simple prototyping

To prepare for this activity you need to have explored a design problem such as the one found in Activity 8. You will also need to have explored a few of the prototyping tools introduced earlier in this chapter. In this activity the aim is to produce a 'rapid prototype' quickly and easily that simulates the interactive design so that users can use it and give feedback. Because it is a prototype, there is no need to devote time or effort to make the back-end technology work. Where dynamic data is required, such as search results, this can be replaced by static data. If you find that something is difficult to simulate in the prototype, then it can be left out and its function explained to the user at the point where they encounter it.

If you are sceptical about the benefits of prototyping then we urge you to give it a try. It is a step toward participatory design and for some designers it may seem like relinquishing control. In reality, it will validate the hard work done in researching and specifying the design and save huge amounts of wasted time and money on designs that simply do not work as well as they should.

Design and amending the activity

We have designed this activity so that it can be done using little more than pencil, paper and Scotch Magic Tape. The interface and elements at every stage are sketched on individual pieces of paper or thin card. It may save time to create the elements in software and print them out, depending on the complexity of the interactions. The prototype is made interactive by an assistant who moves the interface elements in and out of the 'interface' in response to the actions that the user takes. This is a low-tech approach but has the advantage of being really easy to set up, incredibly flexible and less intimidating for some users. We also think that users are more open with their comments because they can see that the prototype is clearly a work in progress. It is easy to make notes on the interface during a user test and to change the flow of interaction if required.

Digital prototype

If you would prefer to create a digital prototype, then there are many online tools that do the job. Some simulate the paper prototyping method by simply presenting the interface on a computer screen, with the option to retain a hand-drawn style. They usually include a library of common interface graphics. More sophisticated prototyping tools include libraries of high-fidelity interface graphics that appear real to the user and offer functions to simulate links and transitions. Some have the additional benefit of being able to run prototype simulations on real devices and for prototypes to be stored in the cloud for remote testing and feedback. Some would argue that testing an interface design away from the computer allows better communication between the designer and the user. Others may say that it is impossible to simulate sophisticated computer interactions like swiping and contextual menus with paper.

Steps

1 – preparation

Review your notes and sketches defining the solution that you created in Activity 8. Make a list of each of the interface elements that are needed to build the solution.

Revisit the user goals that were defined in Activity 8 and work through the prototype to review how the user will achieve each goal and make any adjustments that are necessary for the prototype to work as expected. You will use the prototype to validate the design. For example, the first goal states: 'To be aware of all relevant opportunities as they arise.' A solution for this goal could be to design a status indicator that appears at some stage in the user's interaction. If it has, and the user acknowledges that they have achieved that goal, then no problem! If they continue without understanding the significance of the status indicator then the solution has not been validated. You may find it useful to write a statement of what constitutes success for each goal and refer to it during user testing.

2 – make the interface elements

Cut paper or thin card to the same proportions of a typical device display. These do not need to be the same size as the device display and it may help to make them slightly larger to make the process less fiddly. If colour is required, then this can be applied using crayon shading or by using coloured paper. Draw all the interface elements needed on paper (using the list created in Step 1) and cut them out with scissors.

3 – build

Starting with the user's entry point to the interactive application, position the interface elements and stick them down with magic tape. Consider all user choices available at the entry point and create cards designed to replace the current card for each of the choices that can be made. Alternatively, work at the element level and create a stack of different elements that the assistant can apply to the current card to update it in response to the user's choice. Continue in this way to build the prototype until it is complete.

4 –try it out

Potential problems in the design of the original solution are revealed and opportunities for simplifying and enhancing the user experience become more obvious – both major benefits of what should be a quick and very low cost technique. When you have confidence in the design it is important to test it with potential users. Depending on the size and the scope of the project, you will need to organize a session with people in the target groups to explore the prototype and validate the design. It is a good idea to record the session because what users say can contain a rich source of clues as to how they are responding to the design. Adjust the prototype as required and repeat!

Outcome

This activity should show that an open and enquiring approach to the initial stages of a project's development will save time and produce better results.

◉ uxto.me/a12

Figure 81
UI Stencils supply smart sketching templates and other resources for UX Design teams. These products make the creation of consistent hand-drawn user interface graphics easy and help to get thing moving quickly in the initial stages of prototyping new ideas.

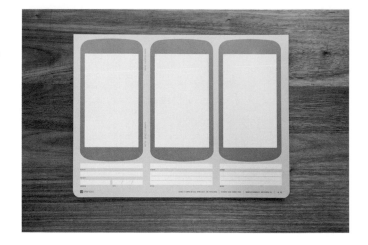

Evaluating tools and resources

Choice

In recent years the availability of software tools designed to help UX Design teams work efficiently has grown enormously. It seems like just about everyone is thinking up new ways to support a UX approach. This sounds great but in reality, there are quite a few tools out there that are not really that useful and others that are so useful that they are 'acquired' by bigger companies and shut down. This is what happened to Pixate in 2016, a promising prototyping tool that came to Google's attention. It is great that new tools are appear constantly on the horizon but before we get too excited let's remember that:

(a) every new tool has a learning curve and needs to be evaluated to ensure that it is up to the job and
(b) if a tool disappears or changes functionality then the disruption can cause significant problems for teams, projects and resource management.

For this reason, UX Designers tend to take a conservative approach to using new tools for live projects, only adopting those that offer significant additional benefits. There is also a widely held view that simple techniques characterised by smaller single-purpose tools are inherently less cumbersome and more effective than complex applications. This is important in a field where agility and flexibility are often the key to success.

Because new things are coming along all the time, a textbook like this is not a good place to look for up-to-date information. Instead we invite you to visit our companion website for more current information. A simple link and short review of a tool or other resource does not provide enough information to decide if it is appropriate for your particular project and approach. For this reason, it is a good idea to devise a way to shorten the list of potential tools and apply criteria to simplify the selection process.

To help you do this there is a checklist template on the companion website. We will regularly run the best tools and resources that we find through the checklist, but this is no substitute for doing your own research! The following five criteria are a good place to start.

1. Cost effectiveness

Is the tool cost effective? The cost of a tool or resource should be considered in the context of the potential benefit. Software costing $10k a year is worth the price if it generates business value or savings of a good percentage more than it cost. If you are just starting out then always enquire about educational, limited free licences or free trial periods. If you are a student then ask your tutors if they have applied for institutional licences for the software that you want to use. If you use opensource software, then check the licence to see if there are restrictions on commercial use.

2. Support and documentation

Good technical support, well-written documentation, training materials and a helpful community of experts are all essential. Opensource software is often better supported than commercial software and so it is worth considering this factor against others, including compatibility and functionality.

3. Compatibility

Does the tool or resource fit in with the rest of your workflow? Will it work on your computers and is it easy to transfer data and produce outputs for things like user tests and presentations? Does it include ways to work collaboratively and integrate with planning and communication tools? If it is a cloud-based product then how secure is your data and does the system used comply with data security regulations in your country?

4. Functionality

Does it produce good results? Are all the functions that you need included? Is it bloated with too many features resulting in slow rather than nimble performance? How long would a similar task take without this software or resource? Does using the software lead to lazy practices, samey results and narrow thinking?

5. History

How did the tool or resource come into being? If it is a software version of a traditional process, then how does it improve the process? Who uses it and what benefits does it bring to their work? When was it last updated and how reliable is the company that produces it? Most designers will give plenty of advice and cite reasons for their choice of toolset. If it works for them, there's a good chance it will work for you too.

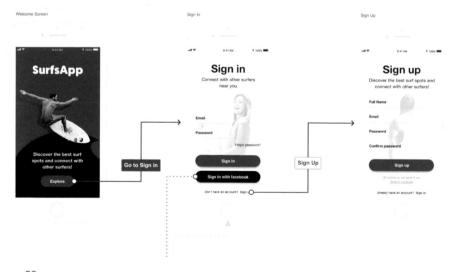

Figure 82
Overflow.io launched their user flow diagramming tool as an early beta programme in mid-2018, giving designers a chance to provide feedback before a full public release.

Conclusion

We hope this book has given you an overview of design for the user experience: the factors of human behaviour and environment that shape our responses to experiences; the designed and constructed elements that contribute to positive experiences; and the tools and methods that designers can incorporate into a working process in order to deliver and assess positive experiences.

This book argues that design is for other people; not for us. Being a more empathetic designer requires that you step out of yourself and recognize that different people have different needs and expectations. We hope this book will encourage you to be innovative in your design responses, and above all to acquire and retain empathy with the end user throughout the design process.

Design for user experience can be driven by thinking about how other people feel, and by reading the existing studies on user behaviour. The real test of our commitment to UX Design will be a willingness to ask real users what they think. By real users, we mean strangers, not friends or classmates or our family. The people close to us are predisposed to say what we want to hear. They will not successfully represent the target demographic.

UX Design is not a simple matter of conforming to international standards or established design processes. It is about respect for the user. Products and services do not have value in themselves. Fxperiences are more important than the products or services themselves, and this has to be considered if we are going to add value to the world with our creative efforts.

A real user has a vested interest in improving the experience of work or play that we are designing for them. The motive of a real user will be to increase their own satisfaction. To this end, they are more likely to tell us things that we need to hear, even if the outcome is more work and different ideas.

For a designer, one of the most intimidating things about UX Design methods is that we are actively inviting other people to be critical of our work and of our ideas. What is more, we may have to leave the comfort of our familiar environment to hear this and respond constructively at all times.

A willingness to take these steps requires the development of character. A thick skin will help and other personal attributes will grow with experience. We will learn courage, resilience, curiosity, humility and critical thinking. These changes in our values as designers will set us apart as the architects of excellent experiences.

We hope this book will encourage you to be innovative in your design responses, and above all to acquire and retain empathy with the end user throughout the design process.

Books

Ambrose, G. and Harris, P. (2018) Layout for Graphic Designers: An Introduction.
Bloomsbury
A visually inspiring book which explains the key principles of layout for the page and, in the new editing, relates these fundamentals to layout for the screen.

Antoniou, G. Groth, P. Harmelen, F. van, and Hoekstra, R. (2015) A Semantic Web Primer.
MIT
One of the most important things about semantics is that the organizational structure that is used must be consistent and have the potential to evolve as new information is incorporated. A Semantic Web Primer thoroughly explains the requirements of such a structure, going into detail about the alternative methods for managing metadata: the hidden 'labels' that define how information is categorized and inter-related.

Barnum, C.M. (2010) Usability Testing Essentials.
Morgan Kaufmann
A readable and pragmatic book about the questions you must ask before researching users and usability, as well as the methods for conducting the research.

Beck, R.C. (2003) Motivation: Theories and principles.
Prentice Hall
A comprehensive reference about human motivation, derived from experiments and observations of human (and animal) behaviour. This book will give an insight into the biological forces that are at the root of our choices and preferences.

Blythe, M.A. and Monk, A. (2018) Funology 2: From usability to enjoyment (second Edition).
Kluwer Academic
A collection of research papers into the relationship between interactions and pleasure. After a useful discussion of the nature of fun, it moves on to more specific case studies of enjoyable interactions between people and technology.

Brown, D.M. (2011) Communicating Design: Developing website documentation for design and planning.
New Riders
A helpful guidebook on professional documentation and presentation. It shows how to organize and format the findings from user research, and the plans for the design and implementation of a product or service.

BS EN ISO 9241-210:2010 Ergonomics of human–system interaction. Human-centred design for interactive systems.
ISO/BSI
The international standard currently most relevant to UXD. It is called Part 210 because it forms just one part of a group of standards within the Ergonomics of Human–System Interaction. Other areas include Part 11: Guidance on usability and Part 920: Guidance on tactile and haptic interactions.

Buxton, B. (2007) Sketching User Experience.
Morgan Kaufmann
Sketching can mean drawing, improvising, prototyping and iterating. Through a series of personal anecdotes and thoughtful case studies, Bill Buxton shows how investigating the user context is a crucial part of the design problem.

Cooper, A., Reimann, R. and Cronin, D. (2007) About Face 3: The essentials of interaction design.
Wiley
A highly recommended read: it explains and promotes a holistic approach to interaction design, and provides detailed, useful guidance on all stages of a UXD process.

Csikszentmihalyi, M. (2000) Beyond Boredom and Anxiety: Experiencing flow in work and play.
Jossey-Bass
Mihaly Csikszentmihalyi (pronounced 'cheek-sent-me-high-yee') has spent decades investigating happiness and motivation. His studies are based upon interviews

with experts, such as mountaineers and concert pianists, who regularly achieve a state of 'flow', in which an activity becomes engrossing and intrinsically motivated. Here, Csikszentmihalyi explains what is required to help create and maintain a flow state.

De Bono, E. (2015) Serious Creativity: A step-by-step approach to using the logic of creative thinking
Vermilion
De Bono has written many books on the principles of Creative Thinking, but this is the most implementable of his books for an individual striving to come up with ideas: a toolkit of simple but productive creative strategies are explained clearly and helpfully.

Garrett, J.J. (2011) The Elements of User Experience: User-centered design for the Web and beyond.
New Riders
The Elements of User Experience deconstructs the experience of using a website into a tier of interactions, from the initial visual appearance of the page down to the underlying business objectives of the website owner. The book provides a clear and universal framework for discussing the user experience with partners in the design process.

Hall, S. (2012) This Means This, This Means That: A user's guide to semiotics.
Laurence King
In a series of intriguing and vividly illustrated questions, this book introduces many of the key ideas of semiotics, as well as the histories of the thinkers behind them. It shows the various ways in which we find (or overlook) the meaning in visual messages.

Koster, R. (2013) A Theory of Fun for Game Design.
O'Reilly Media
A conversational philosophy on why games are fun, and how this can be applied to other interactions.

Krug, S. (2013) Don't Make Me Think!: A common sense approach to Web usability.
New Riders
An often-cited and immensely readable guide to designing usable web-pages, with lots of clear examples of and subtle design changes that can eliminate user anxiety.

Goodman, E., Kuniavsky, M. and Moed, M. (2012) Observing the User Experience: A practitioner's guide to user research.
Morgan Kaufmann
A detailed and reassuring guide to planning, conducting and utilizing user research. The book explains how to select the most appropriate research method, and how to undertake and document the different types of observations and interviews.

Lidwell, W., Holden, K. and Butler, J. (2010) Universal Principles of Design: 125 ways to enhance usability, influence perception, increase appeal, make better design decisions, and teach through design.
Rockport
A principle is something that has been proven, over time, to work. In design studies, some of these principles may be based on science and mathematics, or the ergonomics of how the human body has evolved over millennia. Other established principles arise from our shared exposure to works of art across the centuries. Universal principles of design gather together some of the most fundamental and immutable 'rules of thumb' when designing for human beings, and show how they still apply to emerging platforms and technologies.

Lupton, E. (2010) Thinking with Type: A critical guide for designers, writers, editors and students (second edition).
Princeton Architectural Press
A detailed overview of the history, philosophy, art and science of typography for different media.

Maslow, A.H. and Frager, R. (1987) Motivation and Personality.
Addison Wesley
Maslow was an American psychologist who devised the famous 'hierarchy of needs'. This

is the book in which his model is explained. Usually depicted as a triangle, the model suggests that certain 'lower' physiological needs (such as security and hunger) must be satisfied before 'higher' needs (such as belonging and esteem) can be addressed.

McKee, R. (1999) Story: Substance, structure, style, and the principles of screenwriting.
Methuen
McKee explains how narrative structure can be simplified to a few crucial features, but still provide endless variation. The principles of character, goals and antagonism that McKee discusses in relation to movies can be related to all other types of human experience.

Mulder, S. and Yaar, Z. (2007) The User is Always Right: A practical guide to creating and using personas for the Web.
New Riders
An enthusiastic manifesto and practical guide to personas explaining what they are, why to use them and how to create them.

Nemeth, C. (2004) Human Factors Methods for Design: Making systems human-centered.
CRC Press
A technical guide to designing processes that are sympathetic to the limits of human attention, memory and understanding.

Norman, D.A. (2005) Emotional Design: Why we love (or hate) everyday things.
Basic Books
Don Norman is a prominent champion of user-centred design. This book is a persuasive and entertaining reminder that efficiency and usability are not the only objectives of a user-centred approach; human emotions and aesthetics are also an important part of a positive user experience.

Olins, W. (2008) Wally Olins: The brand handbook.
Thames & Hudson
A visually rich book about why brands matter to businesses and users, and the effort required to create and nurture them.

Porter, J. (2008) Designing for the Social Web.
Pearson Education
This book shows, with many entertaining and clear examples, how social enterprise succeeds when the people behind it are sensitive to the social needs of the users.

Salen, K. and Zimmerman, E. (2004) Rules of Play: Game design fundamentals.
MIT
A very thorough and entertaining textbook about the mechanics, rules and challenges of playing games, and how the intelligent design of games corresponds to aspects of human behaviour.

Snyder, Carolyn (2003) Paper Prototyping: The fast and easy way to design and refine user interfaces.
Morgan Kaufmann
This book explains every last detail of paper prototyping techniques, including what type of sticky tape to use and how to test prototypes with users.

Tufte, E.R. (2001) The Visual Display of Quantitative Information Graphics
Graphics Press
A critical overview of the history of information graphics, it explores the ambiguities and the ethics of translating data into clear and accurate visuals.

Weinman, L. and Karp, A. (2003) Designing Web graphics 4.
New Riders
This book provides many of the answers about how digital images should be planned, formatted and optimized for different platforms. It is an active dialogue that will guide the designer in their design iterations.

Websites

Don Norman Blog
Don Norman is credited with inventing the term 'user experience'. His blog includes articles about designing for people, and information about his books and appearances at international events.
www.jnd.org

Smashing Magazine
A web magazine about all aspects of UXD, from user research and client liaison, to coding and development for specific platforms.
www.smashingmagazine.com

Stack Exchange: User Experience
The world is full of people who have learned the hard way, so that you do not need to! Stack Exchange is a forum where experienced designers will respond to questions about user experience design.
ux.stackexchange.com

The UX Booth
A blog of articles about user experience, usability, research, design tools, and working with clients.
www.uxbooth.com

W3CStandards
The World Wide Web Consortium (W3C) is an organization that works to define international standards for web development. It is the W3C that arbitrates what is 'valid' in terms of web applications and communications. Its standards page has the latest information about proposed standards for the emerging platforms and technologies.
www.w3.org/standards

Web Content Accessibility Guidelines (WCAG)
The Web Content Accessibility Guidelines provide guidance on considering accessibility in design projects for the web, but the principles can be applied to other experiences.
https://www.w3.org/WAI/intro/wcag

The online companion for this book offers easy access to learning resources designed to help students and teachers of UX Design.
uxto.me

A–B Testing This testing method compares two variants of the same website or app. The 'B' version of the website would typically have only one distinct difference to the interface of the 'A' version, such as a 'call-to-action' that is a different colour, shape or position. By comparing the conversion data from the two sites, designers can see which of the two was most effective, and iterate accordingly.

Aesthetics Those features that we perceive as being beautiful, or not. Aesthetics are often considered as important as other factors in the user's experience.

Agile Development An iterative approach to developing software that strives to make prompt, incremental improvements to software based upon changing circumstances and evolving design requirements.

Analytics Monitoring the traffic to websites generates tremendous amounts of complex data. Analytics are a tool for harvesting data and presenting it in various ways as readable graphs.

Antagonism A force of opposition in a story or game, typically a 'bad guy', a time constraint, or a force of nature.

Augmented Reality (AR) A technology that can detect images via the camera in digital devices, and then superimpose context-specific media onto the image.

Back-end The hidden 'machinery' of a system that the user does not directly encounter, but which is still required for the experience to function. See also 'Front-end'.

Behavioural A type of emotional human response. In UX Design, behavioural responses are the ones that we feel when occupied with using a product or service.

Brainstorming An approach to problem solving and idea generation. The strategy is to rapidly generate as many solutions as possible without judgement, and then, only once this ideas phase is over, move on to evaluate them more soberly.

Card-sorting A research method in which a user is given a stack of cards with key terms written on them. The user is asked to sort the cards into logical groups, creating an organizational structure that makes sense to them. The test is repeated with multiple users to reveal patterns of consistent behaviour and expectation.

Causality The principle describing how actions are understood to have logical consequences.

Competitive Advantage The features and benefits of a service or product that sets it apart from its competitors, as well as the corporate strategy of identifying and exploiting these features and benefits.

Context The diverse set of circumstances that surround and impact upon an experience.

Conversion An action by a user that represents some kind of commitment to a product or service. A visitor to a website is 'converted' if they respond to a 'call to action', which may be to subscribe to a service or choose a product.

Copyright A collection of protective laws that grant a creator some control over how a literary or artistic work may be used. Computer code is protected as a 'literary' work. Copyright can be traded.

Creative Commons A licensing system for digital media. A creator can attach a Creative Commons license to a digital work (such as a photograph or a music track) to make clear whether or not the work may be freely used elsewhere.

CSS – Cascading Style Sheets Whereas HTML is the mark-up language that defines the content and structure of a webpage, CSS is the coding language used to describe the visual elements, including position, scale and colour.

Demographic A group of people with a common characteristic, such as age or gender; often used to describe a target group of users.

Empathy The human capacity to understand how other people feel.

Ergonomics A discipline of design and engineering that studies the relationship between people and their surroundings.

Ethnography A type of observational research that observes subjects in their normal environment.

Extrinsic External to, or beyond itself. 'Extrinsic' is a term that can be applied to human motivation, meaning that the user undertakes a task in response to external pressures or influences.

Eye-tracking See Gaze-tracking

Flow According to psychologist Mihaly Csikszentmihalyi, flow is the mental state of somebody who is fully immersed in a focused activity.

Focus Group A selection of target users who are assembled by a researcher or designer in order to share their ideas and opinions about design problems and solutions.

Front-end The 'front-end' of a product or service is the 'surface': the aesthetics; the typography, imagery and interaction design that provide the user with direct sensory cues. See also 'Back-end'.

Gantt Chart A project management tool devised by engineer Henry Gannt: a timeline which shows the sequence and interdependencies of all the discrete tasks within a larger project.

Gaze-tracking Gaze-tracking (or eye-tracking) is a technology that records the precise direction of your gaze. In user testing, gaze-tracking can identify the areas of a visual display that capture the user's attention.

Gestalt Gestalt is a field of human psychology that attempts to explain how we make sense of visual information.

Goal A specific objective to be accomplished, a goal may help define the requirements of an experience, or provide a benchmark for user testing.

Haptic Anything related to the sense of touch. Haptic technologies are those that are designed to provide some kind of touch-based interface or feedback.

Hierarchy A hierarchy is an organizing structure in which people, information or objects are arranged by rank or importance: the most significant appear at the top, and the least are found at the bottom.

HTML – Hypertext Mark-up Language HTML is the mark-up language that describes how the content of a webpage should be organized and hyperlinked.

Icon In the field of semiotics, an icon is a particular type of sign that has some kind of resemblance to the thing it signifies.

Index In the field of semiotics, an index is a particular type of sign that points to, or indicates, something else that has meaning or purpose, such as a depression in a surface indicating a good place to put your thumb.

Information Architecture The principle of specifying how a mass of information should be logically arranged, navigated and extended.

Intellectual Property (IP) Any creative work protected by copyright. Because creators can sell licenses allowing their copyrighted work to be reused, Intellectual Property is a valuable commodity that is carefully managed and protected.

Intrinsic Belonging to, or contained within, itself. 'Intrinsic' is a term that can be applied to human motivation, meaning that the user undertakes a task with no external pressure or influence.

Intuitive Intuition is the sensation of immediate understanding that does not require any form of instruction, interpretation or prior experience. In truth, there is no such thing as an intuitive experience, as all new encounters will rely on existing knowledge and experience.

ISO – International Organization for Standardization An international body that defines global standards of safety and quality.

Iteration A process of repetition. In UX Design, the aim of repeating the process is to continuously and successively improve upon the previous version of the design.

Metadata Data about data. It often accompanies digital media in order to provide extra information, such as technical data or content description.

Metaphor Something familiar referred to in a different context to help make sense of something unfamiliar.

Mnemonics A kind of encoding pattern or system of recognition used to make more complex information more memorable. 'One collar, two sleeves' is a mnemonic to recall the correct number of specific consonants in the word 'necessary'.

Persona A persona is a fictitious character created when considering the suitability of a design solution for an archetypal user. Personae are based upon research into real people, rather than an imagined 'ideal' user.

PET Design – Persuasion, Emotion, Trust A methodology for UX research and design centred on the psychology of human behaviour, pioneered by Human Factors Inc.

Platform An underlying system or infrastructure, such as an operating system (Windows, Android or Symbian). Because ubiquitous web-based tools (Facebook, Twitter) are not loyal to specific hardware technologies or operating systems, these can also be regarded as independent platforms.

Protagonist The 'hero/heroine' of a narrative.

Prototype A mock-up or early build of a product or service, developed quickly to illustrate a design concept, or so that it can be used in testing in order to define exactly what type of refinements are required.

Qualitative Statistical data concerned with the immeasurable, such as the opinions of users.

Quantitative Statistical data that is measurable and comparable, such as the numbers of visitors to a website.

Rapid Prototyping A method of using very simple materials, or specialist design templates, in order to quickly produce a working prototype so that a design concept can be tested.

Reflective A type of emotional human response. In UX Design, behavioural responses are the ones that we feel when occupied with using a product or service.

Responsive Design An approach to digital design that enables information to be supplied to a target device in a format that adapts to its display characteristics.

Scenario A story (or scene) that describes a set of circumstances (see also persona and context).

Schema A model or structure of information that is created by, and for, the individual's mind. Schemata are our own personal information architectures.

Semantics The science and study of 'meaning'. In UX Design, it describes a conscious effort to organize information in a way that users will find meaningful.

SEO – Search Engine Optimization A strategic attempt to make webpages highly visible to relevant searches made with search engines such as Google. A number of techniques are used, including embedding key words into the HTML of the page, as well as maximizing the number of other links to the website from elsewhere.

Stakeholders A person or organization with an interest in a project or who may be affected by the existence of a project.

Symbol In the field of semiotics, a symbol is a particular type of sign that has a completely arbitrary and negotiated relationship with thing it signifies, such as a red light signifying 'stop'.

Task Modelling A UX Design methodology that attempts to recognize the way that people approach a real-world objective (or task), and designing experiences to accommodate this task-oriented approach.

Tree Testing This is a technique used to test a proposed information architecture. The test participant is given a search term, and then descends the hierarchy of the information architecture, selecting from the available categories (or 'branches') at each level, in pursuit of the search term. If the structure is appropriate, the user should arrive at the target item with few detours.

UCD – User Centred Design An iterative approach to design that involves the end user at various stages of the design process in order to create a system that is sensitive to their environment and the tasks they need to accomplish.

UI – User Interface The designed space in which an interaction occurs between a user and a system or product.

Usability The extent to which a designed experience is found to be usable by its intended users.

Usability Testing The process of testing and assessing a product or service in order to discover how usable it is for the intended users.

UX – User Experience How a designed system affects the user and elicits feelings and attitudes that remain associated with that system.

Validation The process of checking that something meets predetermined criteria or a set of rules.

Values Standards that determine what we believe to be important or correct and influence how we act.

Visceral A type of emotional human response. In UX Design, visceral responses are the 'gut' feelings that we have before we consider the experience on an intellectual level.

W3C – World Wide Web Consortium An international community that develops open standards to ensure the long-term growth of the Web.

Wireframes A scheme for depicting the planned arrangement of key elements in an interface design. The plan will omit fine details and specific content, replacing these with a lattice of empty rectangular placeholders, in order to show only the underlying visual hierarchy of the interface.

Figure 1: Design - Bar: Adam Gill, Packaging: Socio Design, Photography: Bo San Cheung, Company, Beau Cacao

Figure 2: © Authors

Figure 3: © Authors

Figure 4: Photo by Roberto Nickson (@g) on Unsplash

Figure 5a: © Osmo / Crieghton Vance / Karen O'Dell

Figure 5b: © Osmo / Crieghton Vance / Karen O'Dell

Figure 6: © Courtesy of Carol Smith, carolsmithphotography.com

Figure 7: Dominique A. Pineiro

Figure 8: © Authors

Figure 9: © Authors

Figure 10: © Authors

Figure 11: © Authors

Figure 12: © Authors

Figure 13: © Authors

Figure 14a: Tony Hobba Architects

Figure 14b: Tony Hobba Architects

Figure 15a: © Courtesy of Urban Screen, urbanscreen.com

Figure 15b: © Courtesy of Urban Screen, urbanscreen.com

Figure 15c: © Courtesy of Urban Screen, urbanscreen.com

Figure 16: Oskar Krawczyk - unsplash

Figure 17a: Jordi Parra, Umea Institute of Design 2011

Figure 17b: Jordi Parra, Umea Institute of Design 2011

Figure 17c: Jordi Parra, Umea Institute of Design 2011

Figure 18a: © Courtesy of Preloaded, preloaded.com

Figure 18b: © Courtesy of Preloaded, preloaded.com

Figure 18c: © Courtesy of Preloaded, preloaded.com

Figure 19: Edgar Allanwood

Figure 20a: © Courtesy of Michael Hansen, michaelhansenwork.dk

Figure 20b: © Courtesy of Michael Hansen, michaelhansenwork.dk

Figure 20c: © Courtesy of Michael Hansen, michaelhansenwork.dk

Figure 21a: © Duolingo

Figure 21b: © Duolingo

Figure 21c: © Duolingo

Figure 22a: Rahul Thanki (rspb-images.com)

Figure 22b: Rahul Thanki (rspb-images.com)

Figure 22c: Rahul Thanki (rspb-images.com)

Figure 22d: Rahul Thanki (rspb-images.com)

Figure 23a: Matterport

Figure 23b: Matterport

Figure 24a: © Ben Davies

Figure 24b: © Ben Davies

Figure 24c: © Ben Davies

Figure 25a: © Courtesy of Preloaded, preloaded.com / National Museums Scotland

Figure 25b: © Courtesy of Preloaded, preloaded.com / National Museums Scotland

Figure 25c: © Courtesy of Preloaded, preloaded.com / National Museums Scotland

Figure 26: © Authors

Figure 27a: © Nikita Konkin

Figure 27b: © Nikita Konkin

Figure 28a: © Brave UX LLC

Figure 28b: © Brave UX LLC

Figure 29a: Work by Rotate°

Figure 29b: Work by Rotate°

Figure 29c: Work by Rotate°

Figure 30a: © Courtesy of Preloaded, preloaded.com

Figure 30b: © Courtesy of Preloaded, preloaded.com

Figure 31: © Authors

Figure 32: © Authors

Figure 33: © Authors

Figure 34: © Authors

Figure 35: © Authors

Figure 36: © Authors

Figure 37: © Robowolf

Figure 38a: © Brave UX LLC

Figure 38b: © Brave UX LLC

Figure 38c: © Brave UX LLC

Figure 39a: © 2010, iamgavin.com, all rights reserved

Figure 39b: © Courtesy of Aecom (Strategy Plus), aecom.com

Figure 40: © Authors

Figure 41: © Authors

Figure 42: © Authors

Figure 43: © Authors

Figure 44: Cog Design

Figure 45: © Courtesy of Cog

Figure 46: © Authors